# Herbert Smith Freehills
# PORTRAIT AWARD 2024



NATIONAL PORTRAIT GALLERY

# Contents

# Director's Foreword

Just over a year since the National Portrait Gallery's reopening, we are thrilled to welcome back our Portrait Award with a new sponsor Herbert Smith Freehills. This inaugural year of sponsorship builds on twenty years of support from Herbert Smith Freehills, and continues the Gallery's ambition of ensuring free access to this exhibition.

Exploring the best of contemporary portrait painting, the *Herbert Smith Freehills Portrait Award* showcases works from artists from around the world. This year, we received 1,647 entries from artists in 62 different countries. We hope that our selection of shortlisted and prizewinning works provides inspiration and opportunities for a new generation of talented portraitists.

Reviewing all of the entries in person following the initial digital judging session is always one of the most engaging parts of the competition. The anonymity applied to this process encouraged each of the judges to consider every portrait according to what resonated with them the most. This ranged from the artist's technical ability, to their use of symbolism and narrative, and their application of colour, texture and shadows. The works incited interesting debate amongst the judges before we decided on a final shortlist of 50 works, including 4 prizewinners.

I would like to congratulate the First Prize winner Antony Williams for their portrait *Jacqueline with Still Life*. In this work, Williams creates a striking and enigmatic image combining his interest in still life with the portrait subject. This year's Second and Third Prizes have been awarded to Isabella Watling and Catherine Chambers respectively for their empathetic and well-balanced portraits. Our congratulations also go to Rebecca Orcutt, the winner of this year's Young Artist Award for their painting *Before it's Ruined (or an Unrealized Mean Side)*.

I would like to thank the staff of the National Portrait Gallery for their creativity and commitment to the award, exhibition and accompanying publication, and White Wall Company for brilliantly managing the judging process. I would like to extend my thanks to my fellow judges for providing great input and perspective: Tanya Bentley, Tom Shakespeare, Russell Tovey and Barbara Walker. We are pleased to be celebrating the forty-second edition of such a prestigious award, and to be presenting the exhibition in the newly refurbished Gallery spaces.

We are thankful to Herbert Smith Freehills' contribution to the success of this competition and exhibition.

Dr Nicholas Cullinan OBE
Director, National Portrait Gallery, London

# Sponsor's Foreword

The *Herbert Smith Freehills Portrait Award* showcases the very best in contemporary portrait painting, globally. I am delighted that Herbert Smith Freehills has extended our long term relationship with the National Portrait Gallery as the new sponsor of the Portrait Award.

Access to the art world is often challenging. We are, therefore, pleased to support the Gallery in offering free entry to the annual exhibition, allowing everyone to celebrate the artworks that have been carefully chosen by the judges. Removing barriers to participation and increasing the reach of the Award ensures that many more people can enjoy and benefit from the artworks on display.

This year, the 50 shortlisted works demonstrate portraiture's power to embrace diversity through human-led narratives. I am personally struck by the truths that each artist has boldly depicted on canvas. Such variety can inform an audience's worldview, increasing appreciation of the world around us.

The National Portrait Gallery's Collection gives us a glimpse into the past – a visual snapshot of history and insight into some of the people who have shaped it. It is also about the future. Similarly, our relationship with the Gallery is an enduring one. We have been a sponsor since 2004 and have supported numerous world-class exhibitions, alongside being the Gallery's reopening partner following the most significant redevelopment in their history. We are delighted to continue our partnership now as sponsor of the *Herbert Smith Freehills Portrait Award* and to share the exhibition in the newly refurbished National Portrait Gallery. I hope that every visitor will enjoy the selected artworks for this year's Portrait Award and will join me in congratulating all of the exhibited artists.

Justin D'Agostino MH
Chief Executive Officer, Herbert Smith Freehills

# The Judges

### Russell Tovey
**Actor, author and podcast co-host**

As an actor I've always been drawn to portraiture, to body language and facial expressions. I also feel that it's important for everybody, no matter who they are, to be able to see themselves represented on gallery walls. It has been a privilege, and an exciting opportunity, to discover some very brilliant, underrepresented artists.

### Barbara Walker
**Artist**

The artworks submitted for this year's *Herbert Smith Freehills Portrait Award* were absolutely captivating. Throughout the judging process the artworks revealed remarkable range and complexity, combining modern and classical techniques. The enduring appeal of portraiture in contemporary artistic expression was evident and it was truly inspiring to witness such a vibrant and dynamic theme being explored by artists.

### Tom Shakespeare
**Sociologist and bioethicist**

It was a fascinating day, when judging the artworks, and I learned a lot about portraiture. I think it was interesting how much unanimity occurred between five very different judges. There are clichés – the innocent child and the wise older person – but I was looking for strong images which offered a deeper insight beyond expectations.

### Tanya Bentley
**Contemporary Curator, National Portrait Gallery**

It was thrilling to see so many different approaches to portraiture, from meticulously painted and pre-thought compositions to more serendipitous images. Across the selected works, there is a sense of departure from the formalities traditionally associated with the painted portrait, and instead there is a focus on getting to the heart of the encounter between artist and sitter.

### Dr Nicholas Cullinan OBE
**Director, National Portrait Gallery**

Portraits spark curiosity about the life and character of the person depicted and raise questions about the time and society in which they are made. This years' submissions saw a focus on 'ordinary' people in their habitual environment. What resonated with me was how the works depicted the realities of humanity and highlighted the diverse perspectives of the artists.

# The Prizes

### First Prize

## Antony Williams

Williams' portrait creates a complex relationship between portraiture and still life through a dynamic composition and use of light (p.8).

### Second Prize

## Isabella Watling

In *Zizi*, Watling merges past and present, contrasting classical Renaissance techniques with contemporary modes of fashion (p.10).

### Third Prize

## Catherine Chambers

Depicting a close friend in an intimate moment, Chambers reminds audiences of the complexity of freedom, movement and accessibility (p.12).

### Young Artist Award

## Rebecca Orcutt

Orcutt makes careful use of symbols – the oversized coat and spider web – in their surreal self-portrait to express a moment of fragility and despair (p.14).

The *Herbert Smith Freehills Portrait Award* is open to artists from around the world, aged 18 or over. Exhibited annually at the National Portrait Gallery, London, the Award showcases talented artists, both professional and amateur. The winner of the competition receives £35,000, with second prize receiving £12,000 and third prize £10,000. The Young Artist Award winner, aged between 18 and 30, receives £9,000.

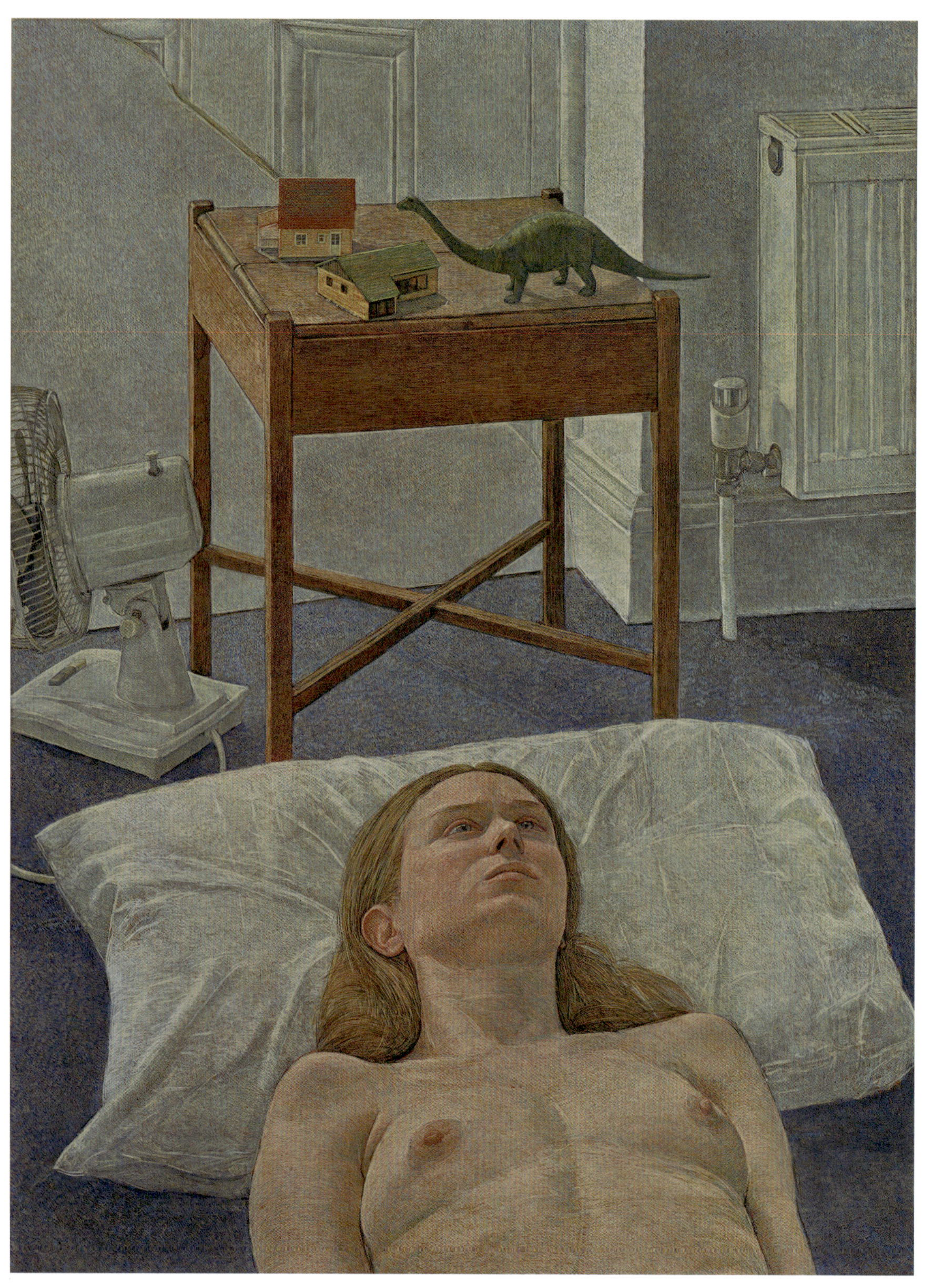

Antony Williams
*Jacqueline with Still Life*, 2020
Tempera on board
1222 × 865mm

# First Prize
# Antony Williams

Winner of the *Herbert Smith Freehills Portrait Award 2024*, Antony Williams has a long association with the National Portrait Gallery, having exhibited at the Portrait Award on eleven occasions, notably in 2017 when he received third prize. This year's winning entry, *Jacqueline with Still Life*, is a portrait of a professional artist's model painted at his former studio on Platts Eyot, an island on the River Thames, shortly before he was forced to move out of the increasingly dilapidated building.

Jacqueline was originally employed as a model by the artist's wife, Caroline Bays, who is also exhibiting at this year's Portrait Award, and was first painted by Williams a decade ago. 'Leaving the studio was a difficult decision as it had provided a lot of inspiration for my work, including the paintings of Jacqueline,' he says. 'I often work with certain models over an extended period. There is something mysterious about Jacqueline's face that fascinates me.'

The portrait was completed over a dozen sittings, with Jacqueline posed in front of his studio's bay window and pictured in natural light reflected off the Thames. 'I could easily have painted her clothed, but I conceived it as a naked portrait partly as a way to convey a vulnerability,' he explains. 'The issue of the male gaze is certainly something a contemporary male artist needs to consider when painting a female model, but I believe it is a tradition that can continue and have relevance if it is approached with respect.'

Williams paints almost exclusively in egg tempera – a quick-drying medium of egg yolk binder, powdered pigments and water that he favours for depicting the subtleties of skin and texture. He begins with a detailed drawing on paper in either charcoal or pencil, which he then transfers onto a gesso panel before applying a painstaking succession of small, deliberate brushstrokes to build up layer upon layer of paint. 'It's a semi-pointillist technique, but a realist way of seeing,' he says.

Having dropped out of art school in the 1980s, Williams is largely self-taught. Living in Chertsey, Surrey, he is currently vice president of the Royal Society of Portrait Painters and his intensely observed compositions are held in collections around the world, including a 1996 portrait of Queen Elizabeth II that caused controversy at the time for its uncompromising representation of ageing and mortality.

Lucian Freud was an early influence, while his most recent paintings signal his regard for the 'strong narrative content' found in Balthus and Paula Rego, as well as a new-found engagement with still life, a consequence of the pandemic when 'it became difficult to work with people'. In 2021, he held his first exhibition of still lifes at Cork Street gallery Messums London, where several works featured the same plastic dinosaur, fan and toy houses that we see in his study of Jacqueline.

'Like some of the people I paint repeatedly, I am now doing the same with objects. For *Jacqueline with Still Life*, my idea was to combine a figure with a still life element but give both equal importance in order to create an implied narrative. Originally, my work was all about observing and recording the truth. Now, I'm more interested in creating narrative elements and moving towards a more surrealist approach.'

Interview by Richard McClure

# Second Prize
# Isabella Watling

Rooted in the artistic traditions of Venetian oil painting, Isabella Watling's courtly and timeless portraits are created by the precise methods and materials that were used in the days of Titian. The London-born artist was taught the centuries-old craft as a student at the Charles H. Cecil Studios, the oldest working private atelier in Florence, Italy, which is dedicated to preserving the classical practice of drawing and painting from life.

Arriving in Italy as a 'blank canvas' in her teens, Watling enthusiastically embraced the sight-size technique, a process dating to the Renaissance and later popularised by the Edwardian society portraits of John Singer Sargent. The subject and easel are placed side by side, allowing the artist to compare them more easily, sight the subject from a distance and then paint it accurately to the scale and proportion of life. 'The beauty and history of Florence felt like a natural place to learn a traditional approach to art,' says Watling. 'The greatest privilege was to be taught by Charles, who has been working there for 40 years, keeping this way of painting alive.'

Viewing her subjects from a distance of five metres, Watling paints straight onto canvas using a limited Venetian colour palette of lead white, ivory black, red vermillion and yellow ochre. 'Sight-size is not just a measuring technique, but a philosophy of seeing,' she says. 'One is constantly walking back and forward to the canvas. If I were to describe it briefly, it would be: looking, mixing, walking, painting, retreating, looking, mixing, walking, correcting, retreating.'

Her prizewinning entry portrays Zizi, a student at a Florence fashion school who had moved to the UK to gain a Masters in textiles. The life-sized portrait was completed over ten sittings at Watling's historic Arts and Crafts home studio in west London, one of several houses built in 1891 for 'bachelor artists' and equipped with high, barrel-vaulted north-facing windows to provide optimal light. 'I was pregnant whilst I painted Zizi and I remember that I was keen to make sure that I finished the painting well before my due date,' she says.

Typically, Watling dresses her sitters in modern clothes, but she chooses pieces that wouldn't look out of place in the sixteenth-century. Here, she bought a gown by fashion designer Simone Rocha, and at times painted the dress arranged on a mannequin in order to reduce the number of sittings. 'I love Simone Rocha's clothes and often try to paint them. I wanted to put a variety of fabrics into the portrait because textiles are the focus of Zizi's studies. The choice of outfit and the textures of the different materials became a way of trying to express a bit of Zizi's personality.'

Watling exhibited at the Portrait Award in 2012 and 2014, and often returns to the Florence atelier to pass on her expertise to a younger generation. 'It's important for me to participate in the life of the school and keep up contact with like-minded painters,' she says. 'I do think that it would be a shame if the Venetian way of painting died out. Whenever I go to the National Gallery, London, there seem to be plenty of visitors who enjoy the Old Masters. I like to think it's not all about the historical significance and that people still take pleasure in the technique as well.'

Interview by Richard McClure

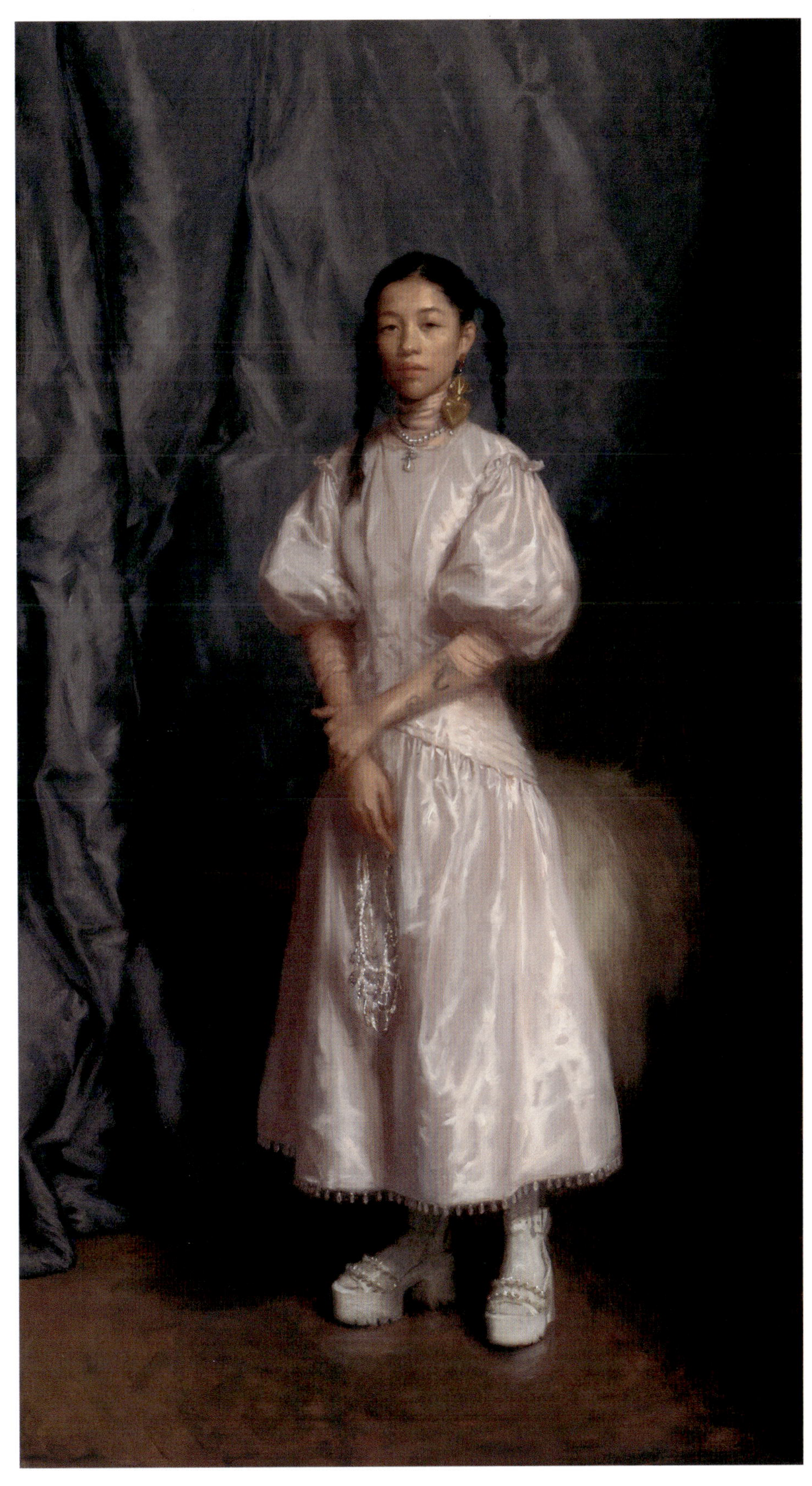

Isabella Watling
*Zizi*, 2023
Oil on canvas
2200 × 1190mm

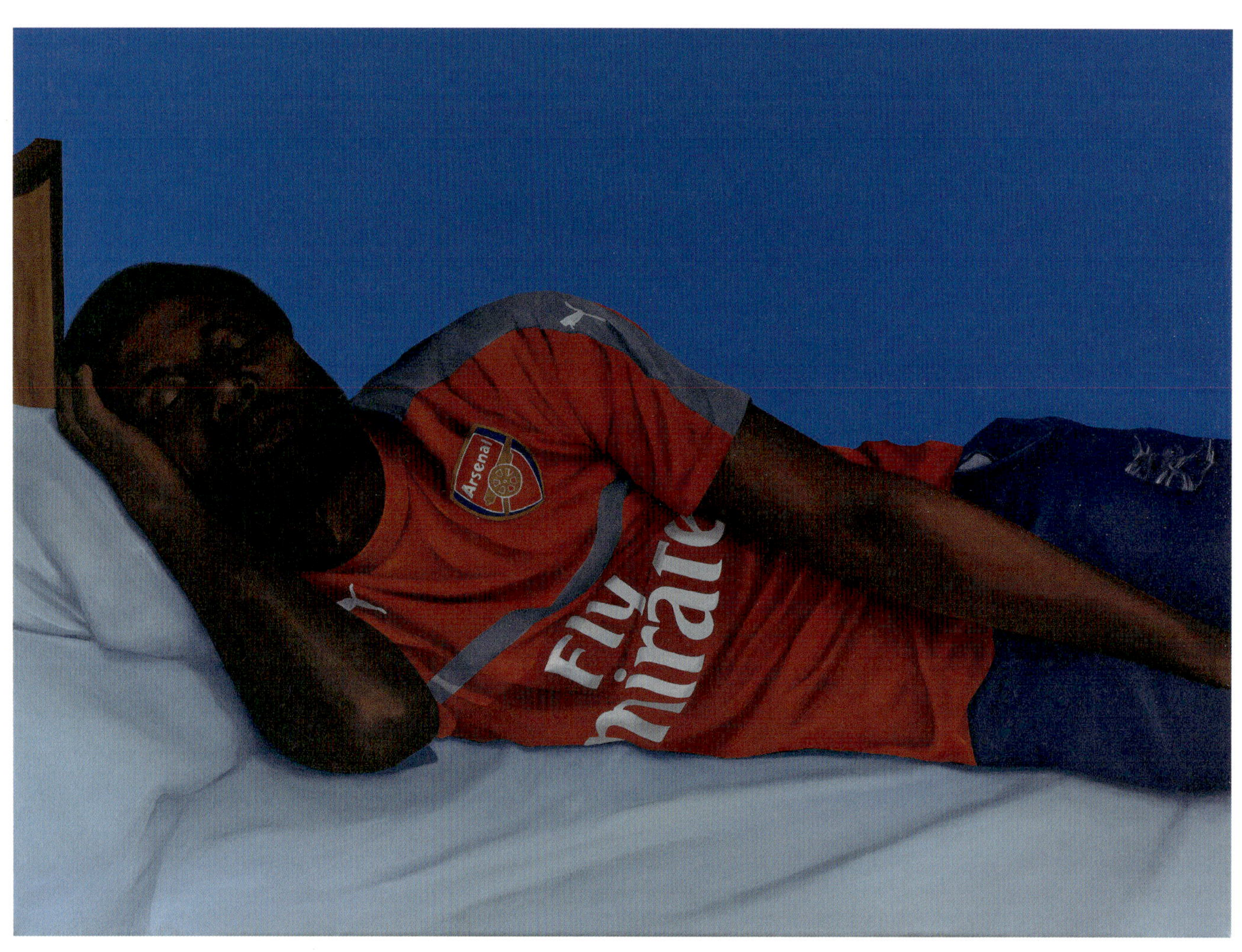

Catherine Chambers
*Lying*, 2020
Oil on canvas
765 × 1010mm

# Third Prize
# Catherine Chambers

A road trip through Africa in 2015 has become an enduring source of inspiration for London-based artist Catherine Chambers. Planning to travel through several countries en route to South Africa, Chambers stopped off at Lalibela in northern Ethiopia, a UNESCO World Heritage site for its rock-hewn churches, and was captivated by the town's ancient culture and the generous welcome she received. 'I became totally involved in Lalibela life and felt as at home there as I have felt anywhere,' she recalls. 'I was meant to stay for a couple of days but I stayed a few months and never made it to South Africa.'

Chambers has returned numerous times and her long-lasting bond with the local community still drives her vibrant, playful portraiture. For her prizewinning entry, *Lying*, she made a series of sketches of a close friend asleep at his family home in Lalibela before developing the idea into a painting when he subsequently visited England. The portrait was completed mostly in one sitting at her studio, with her guest napping on a camp bed, and Chambers painting the surroundings to replicate his bedroom in Ethiopia.

His sleeping figure was a familiar, ready-made composition, she says, and also reflects both the artist and subject's interest in football. 'The Arsenal shirt is important – especially the logo,' she notes. 'A sponsor's products may be entirely inaccessible to the football fan wearing a replica shirt. An airline sponsoring a top European club will not always represent a realistic travel opportunity for a youth in a remote African town. Our friendship regularly reminds us of the stark contrast in freedoms between us, including movement.'

Chambers graduated in 2012 with a degree in drawing from the University of the West of England, and worked solely in pencil until an artist's residency at a north London gallery gave her the impetus to teach herself oil painting.

'Ethiopia was a catalyst in moving to painting, and has undoubtedly influenced my approach to colour. I seem automatically drawn to brighter shades on the palette and avoid introducing pigments that might dull the picture.'

In 2019, she became the first artist to stage a solo show at the Ethiopian embassy in London, an exhibition that included an ongoing series of icons, small works on wood that reference Lalibela's Orthodox Christian tradition. She continues to support her art career with a variety of occupations, taking jobs as a sign writer, mural painter and, currently, as a life skills facilitator running workshops in the UK and abroad. 'I have only ever wanted to be an artist and any other work I undertake is in order to make this possible,' she says. 'All these projects interact with my art; they fuel my interests and bring new stories.'

Lately, Lalibela has been the scene of fighting between local militia and government forces, causing Chambers to shift her creative focus to recent travels around the Persian Gulf. However, her links with Ethiopia remain strong and she intends to go back once the danger has subsided. 'The themes brought to my attention in Lalibela affect people the world over, so my art will continue wherever I find myself,' she says. 'I aim for my work to suggest that foreignness and boundaries are artificial. Ultimately, the more one understands the circumstances of others, superficial differences fade away.'

Interview by Richard McClure

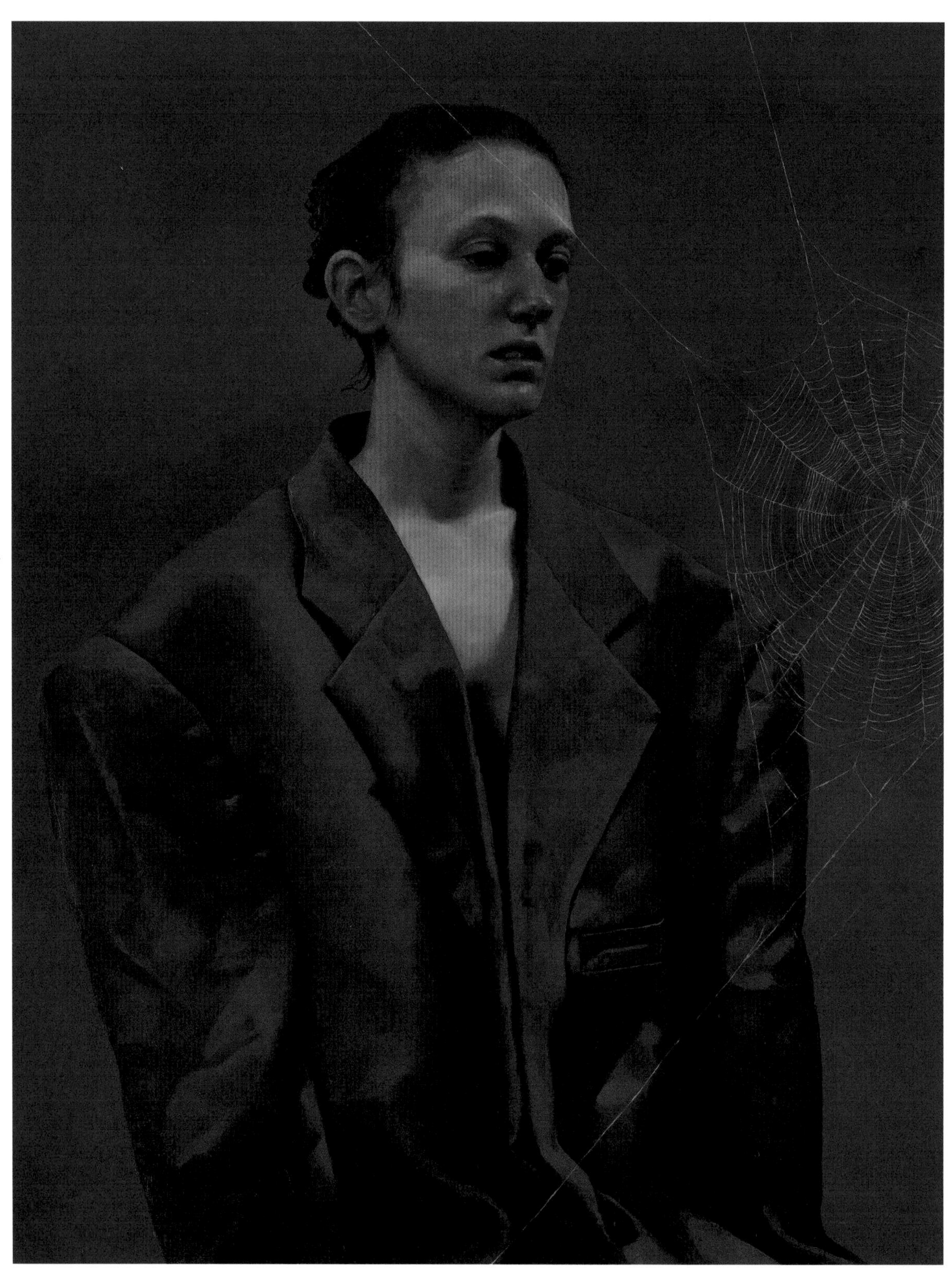

Rebecca Orcutt
*Before it's Ruined (or an Unrealized Mean Side)*, 2020
Oil on canvas
610 × 455mm

# Young Artist Award
# Rebecca Orcutt

Nothing is ever quite as it seems in the portraits and still lifes of American artist Rebecca Orcutt. Her conceptual canvases incorporate a blend of the real and the surreal to create visceral psycho-dramas and scenes that defy everyday logic. Figures wrestle with the vicissitudes of human existence; mundane objects – light switches, microwaves, vending machines – serve as metaphors for our desire to connect with the miraculous and transcendent.

Her work is united by a determination to examine the absurdity of life and how to find or make meaning within it, a tension that lies at the heart of her self-portrait *Before it's Ruined (or An Unrealized Mean Side)?*, for which she has received the 2024 Young Artist Award.

Painted at her studio in North Bend, Washington, the picture reflects a 'specific moment of despair' and questions the lengths we might go to in order to shield ourselves from the pain of potential loss. 'The painting asks whether living with the decision to pre-emptively end something precious is easier than enduring its accidental ruin, even if the cost is genuine connection or love,' explains Orcutt. 'The spider web, with its complicated beauty and fragility, represents the things we dread to lose.'

Quick sketches, colour studies and preliminary drawings of real spider webs laid the groundwork for the painting. For her likeness, she worked from photographs and a mirror, and experimented with different background colours before choosing a blue to reference the azurite pigments of Holbein portraits and the cover of a Magritte monograph on her bookshelf. The creative process also required a thrift-store shopping spree where she bought several men's blazers to try out, finally settling on an oversized jacket that best suited the composition.

'I am drawn to coats; they represent both concealment and exposure – a desire to be seen while fearing the vulnerability of visibility,' says Orcutt, who credits her mentor, artist Jean Sbarra Jones, and her acrylic series of dresses in water, for introducing her to the potential of garments to express intricate emotional themes. Other inspirations include Manet's 'clarity of colour and vivid brushwork', while she attributes the performative aspects of her paintings to her readings of Beckett and Kierkegaard. 'I've moved from faithful realism to constructing scenes more absurd and theatrical,' she notes. 'The aim is less about depicting the world as it is, and more about setting a stage for exploring existential themes.'

Orcutt received a bachelor's degree in painting from Gordon College in Wenham, Massachusetts and a MFA from the New York Academy of Art. She previously exhibited at the Portrait Award in 2015 with a painting entitled *What Now* that depicts a college friend lying prone, his face hidden from view. Indeed, many of Orcutt's portraits feature obscured faces or backs of heads, indicating other core themes of her work – doubt, uncertainty, and aspects of existence that remain unseen.

Partially hiding faces emphasises the inherent limitations in our perception and understanding, she believes. 'The viewer's experience mirrors that of the painting's subjects – grappling with a reality that is only partially revealed to them. It questions if the entirety of a situation, or another person, can ever be fully known. The obscured subjects underscore a narrative of seeking, where the desire to know more is met with the reality that some answers remain perpetually elusive.'

Interview by Richard McClure

# Exhibitors

Kyle Hackett
*After Image*, 2022
Oil on panel
760 × 606mm

Kyle Hackett is an American artist and art professor.
In this self-portrait, he creates a near-silhouetted image
of himself dressed in academic robes. In this staged and
self-aware portrait, Hackett examines the 'Black experience
against my formal position in academia' and considers
W. E. B. Du Bois's concept of 'double consciousness.'
This refers to the experience of being a Black person
in a white-centred world, seeing the world both through
your own eyes and through the white gaze.

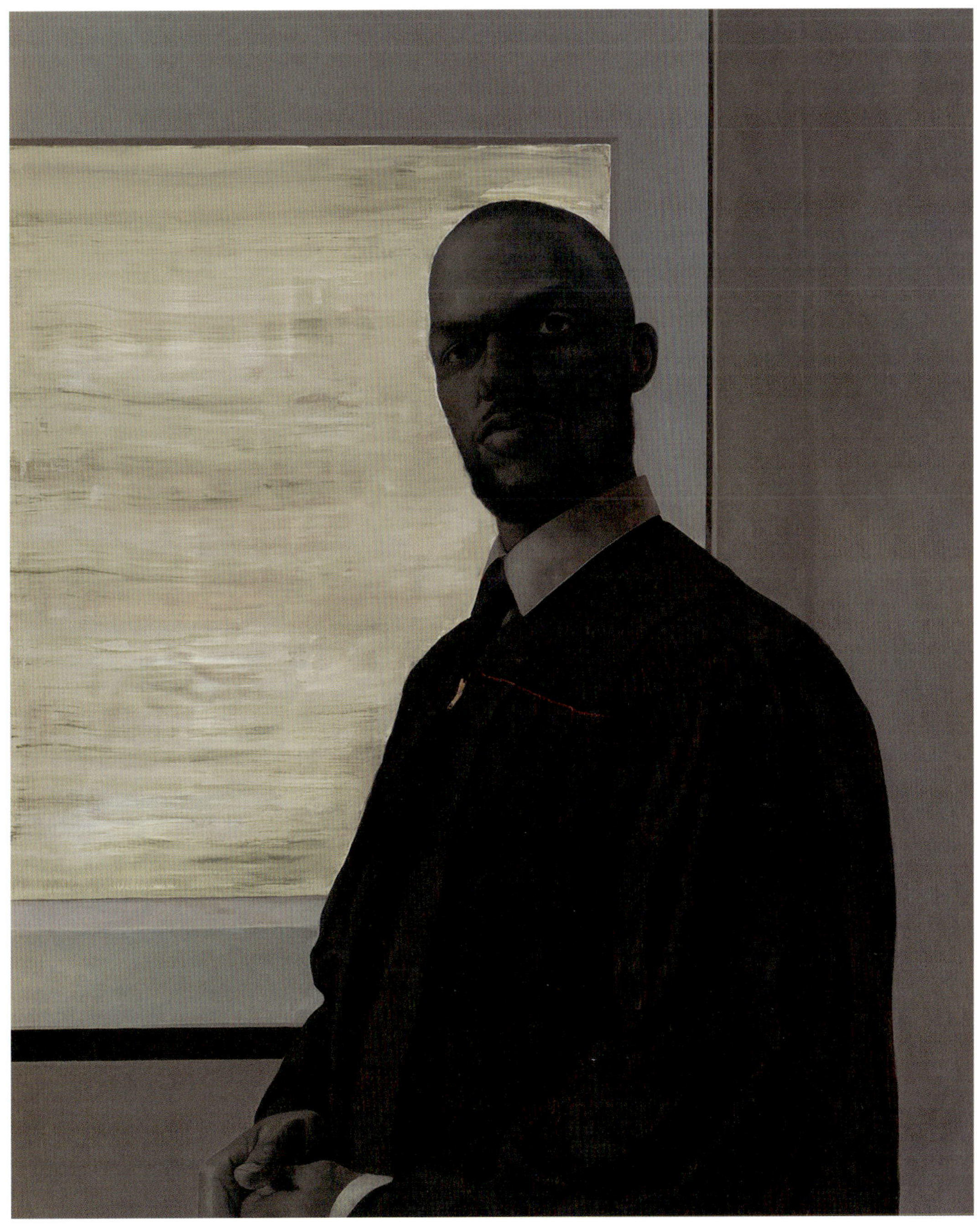

Massimiliano Pironti
*Agnese*, 2023
Oil on aluminium
1070 × 740mm

In this portrait of dancer Agnese, she embraces herself,
her right hand gesturing towards a tattoo on her back
'23.04.2018' – the date she decided to accept her alopecia,
a condition which causes hair loss, and shave off all her
hair. Through the work, Massimiliano Pironti seeks to
question conventional notions of beauty and highlight
Agnese's courage when facing her condition, 'bringing
a new Agnese to the stage of theatre and life.'

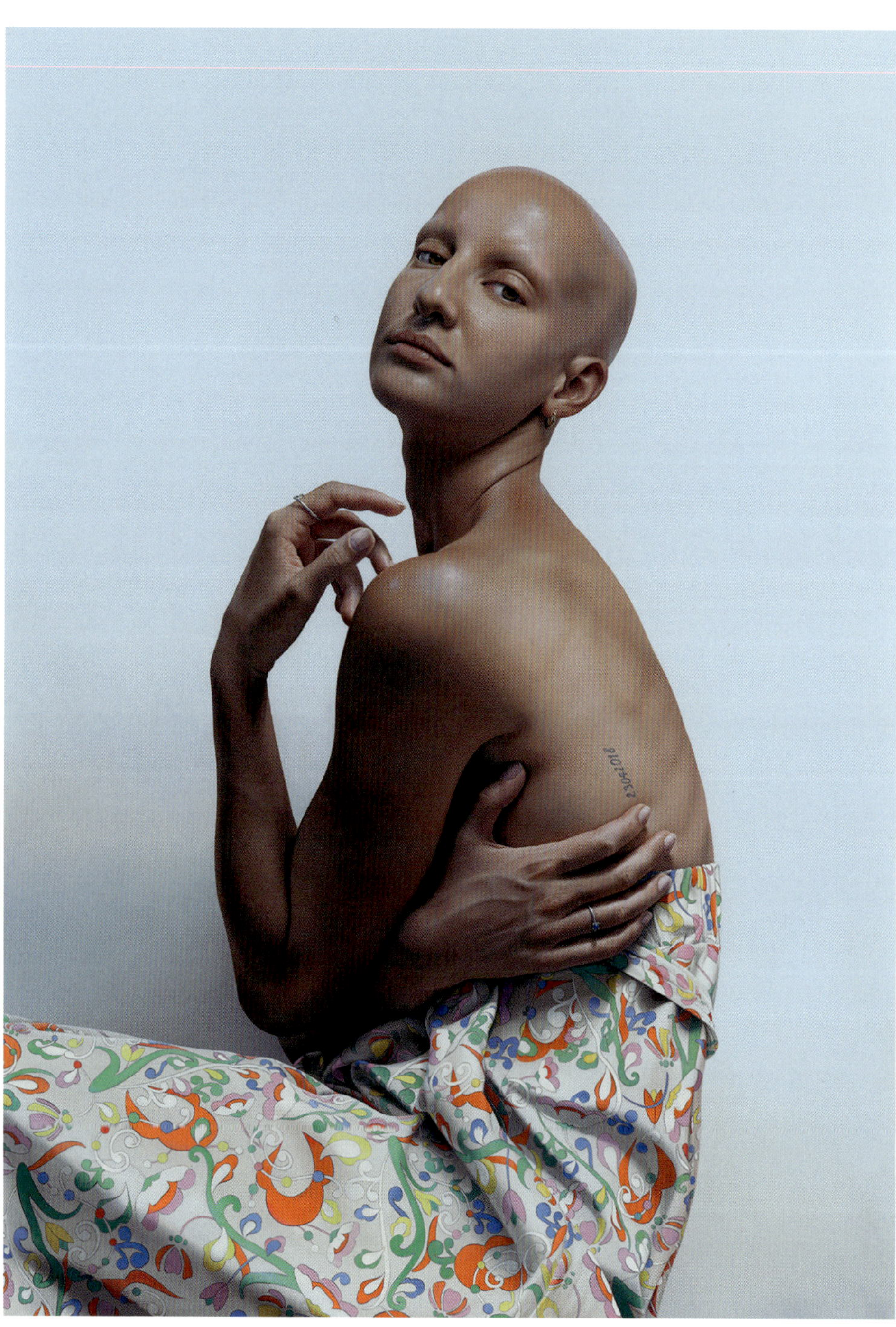

Andrew Norris
*Byuka, Yellow Dress*, 2023
Oil on canvas
800 × 600mm

This portrait of Byuka, a trans non-binary model, was painted from life over several sittings. Andrew Norris tentatively tested out different approaches in paint informed by his many years of studying life drawing. The artist allowed the grey priming to filter through to many elements of the composition such as the head, chest, legs, chair and satin dress, adding a dreamlike quality to the seemingly everyday image.

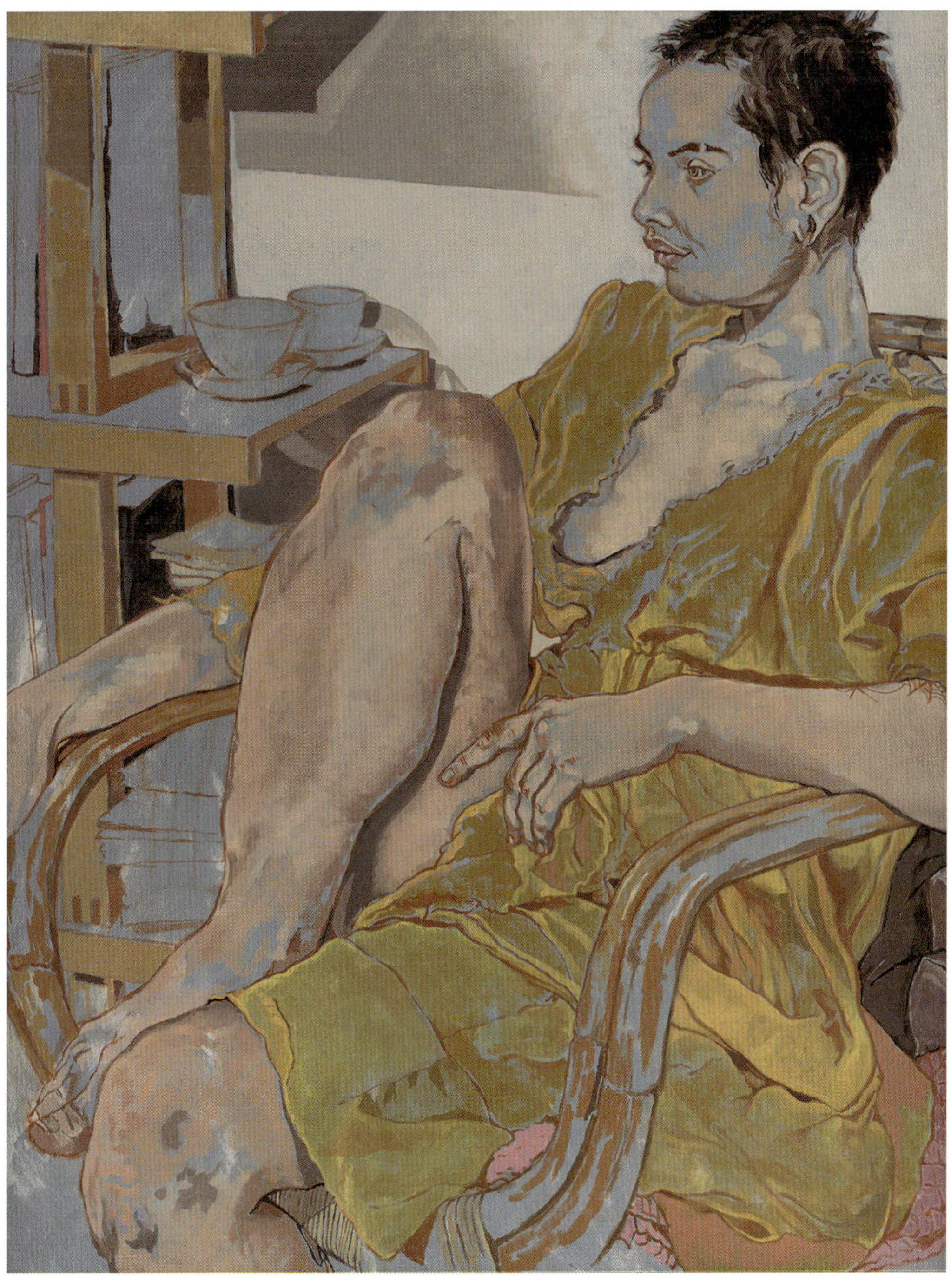

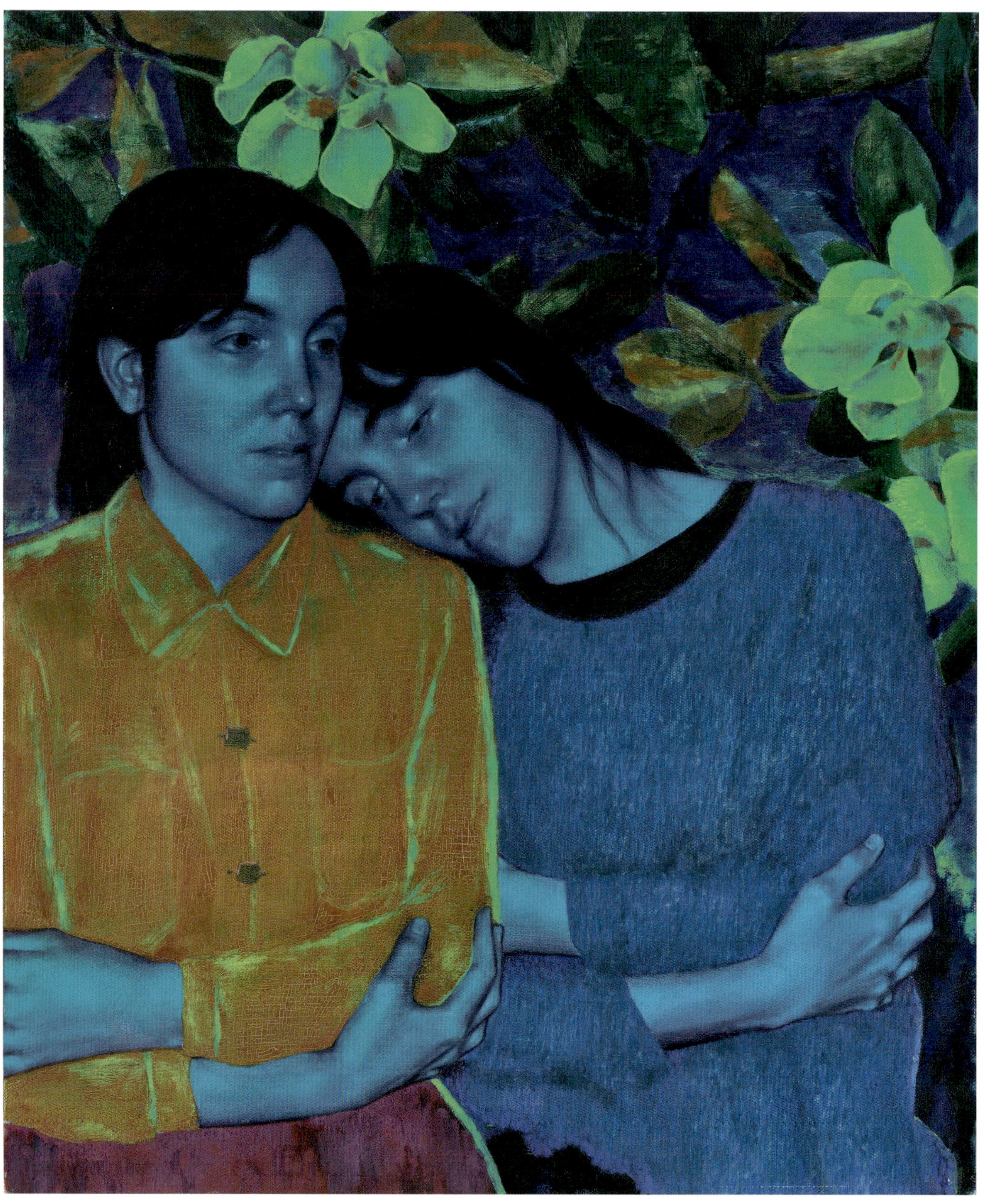

Michael Slusakowicz
*Double Portrait of Clara*, 2021
Oil on canvas
560 × 455mm

Polish-born painter, Michael Slusakowicz, made this
'double portrait' to capture his friend's indecisiveness
when choosing between two university courses. In both
portraits, Clara holds on to herself, whilst her two figures
lean into each other. Slusakowicz explains how 'the painting
came to symbolise one's "self-support" in times of making
significant decisions'. The artist's surreal colour palette,
which he works up by first creating a digital collage of
the image, lends the work an otherworldly quality.

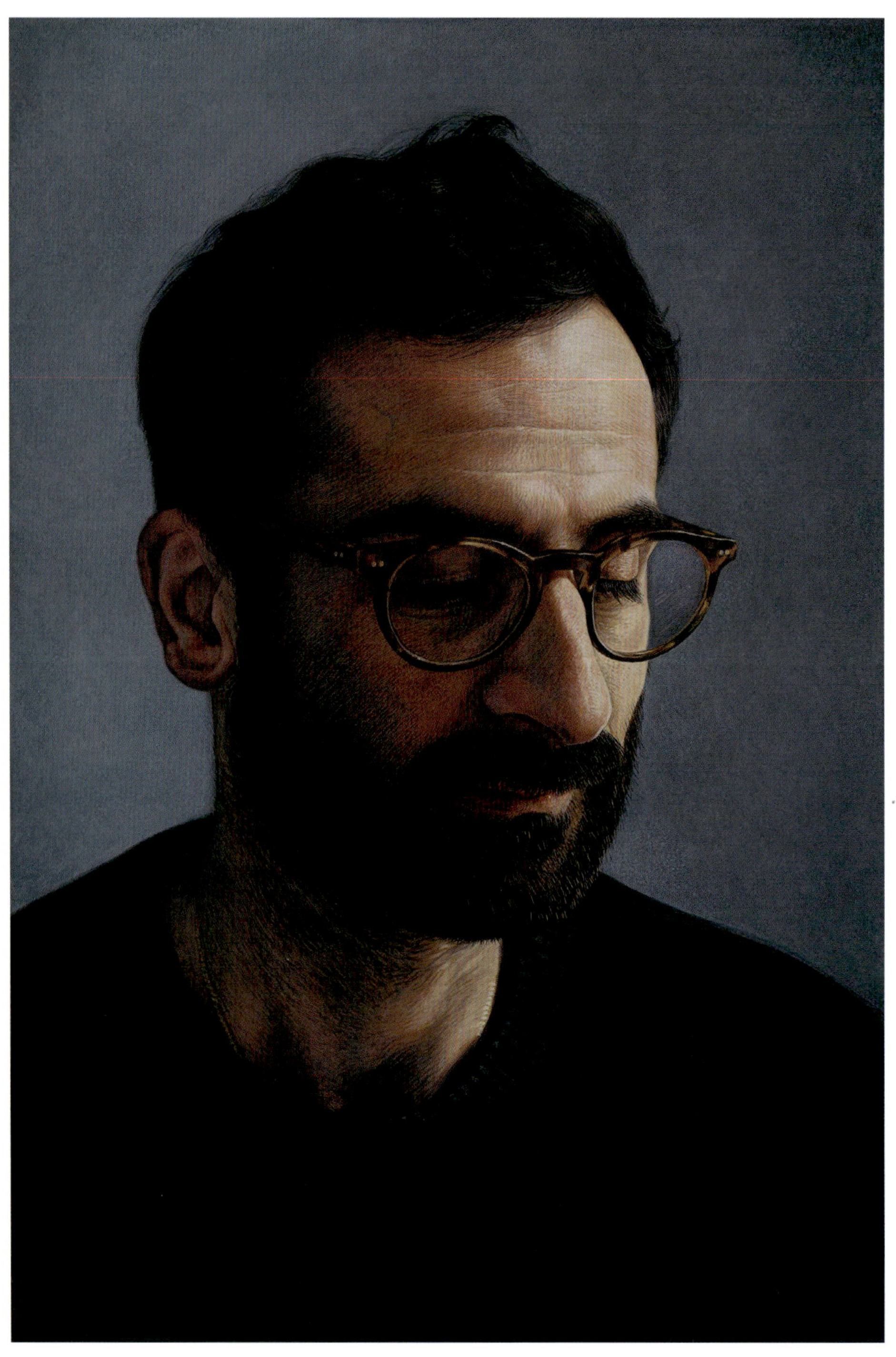

Alan Coulson
*Yianni*, 2024
Acrylic on wood
420 × 300mm

Alan Coulson pieced together this sympathetic portrait from thousands of finely painted brush strokes, still clearly visible on the painting's surface. Having recently formed a friendship with Yianni, the artist asked if he would sit for a portrait aiming to show a 'sensitivity in his nature'. The work is based on an informal sitting at Yianni's home, where Coulson made sketches and took photographs.

George Shapter
*Will & Kenji at Home*, 2020
Oil on board
400 × 600mm

This painting of Will and Kenji with their two dogs, surrounded by houseplants, was made as a wedding gift. George Shapter explains how it 'captures two men beginning to build a life and a home together, in a space that is growing with them'. The seated composition is reminiscent of David Hockney's 1968 double portrait of the American novelist Christopher Isherwood and artist Don Bachardy, in which Bachardy similarly looks on affectionately at his partner whilst Isherwood's gaze remains fixed on the artist.

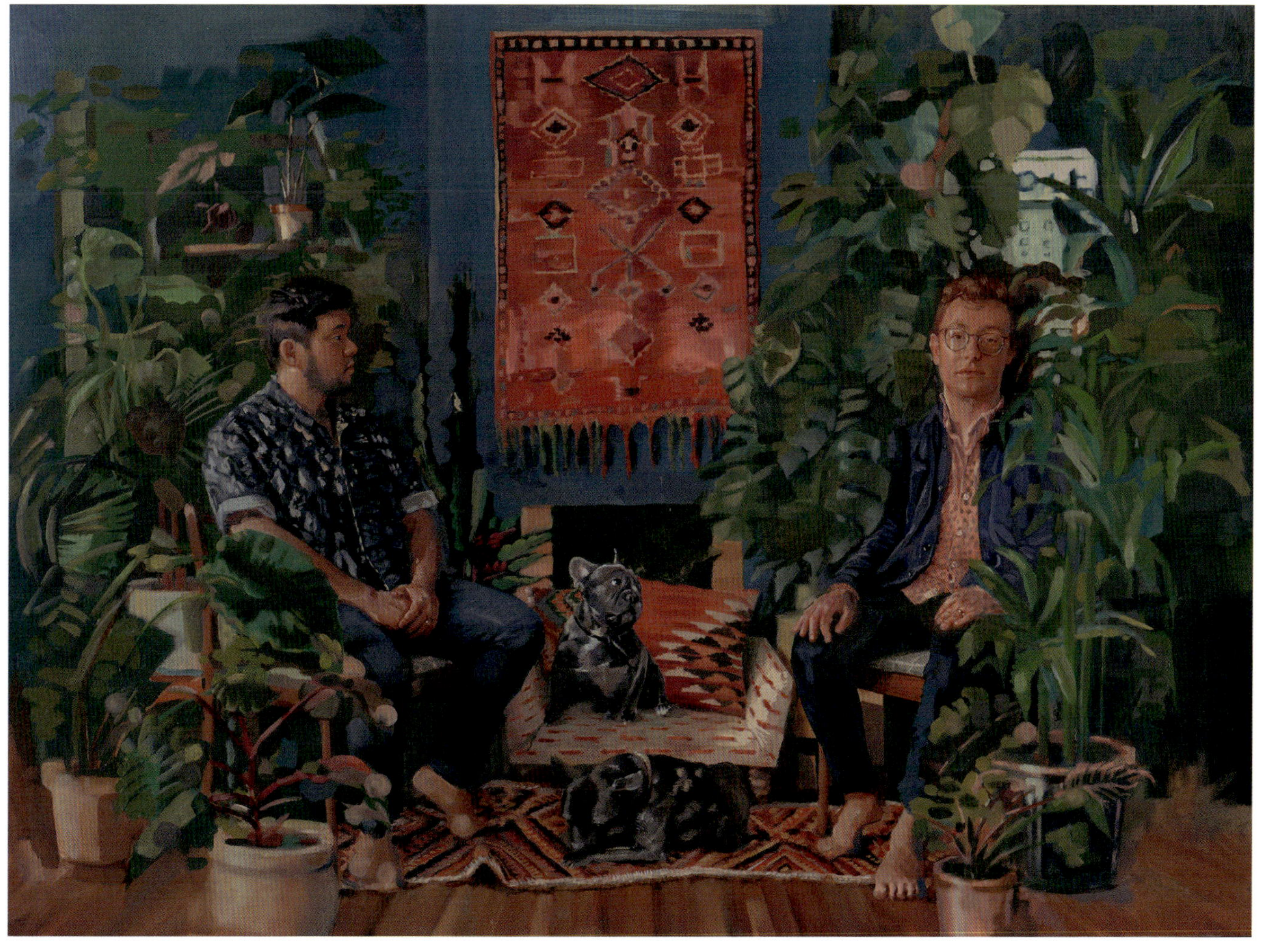

Charlie Ratcliffe
*Callum*, 2023
Oil on canvas
600 × 500mm

Artist Charlie Ratcliffe believes that a familiarity with his
sitter helps him to create paintings with more 'heart'. After
making drawings from life and taking reference photographs,
Ratcliffe worked slowly to produce this contemplative and
well balanced portrait that reflects his friend and fellow
band member's 'strong, but modest' character.

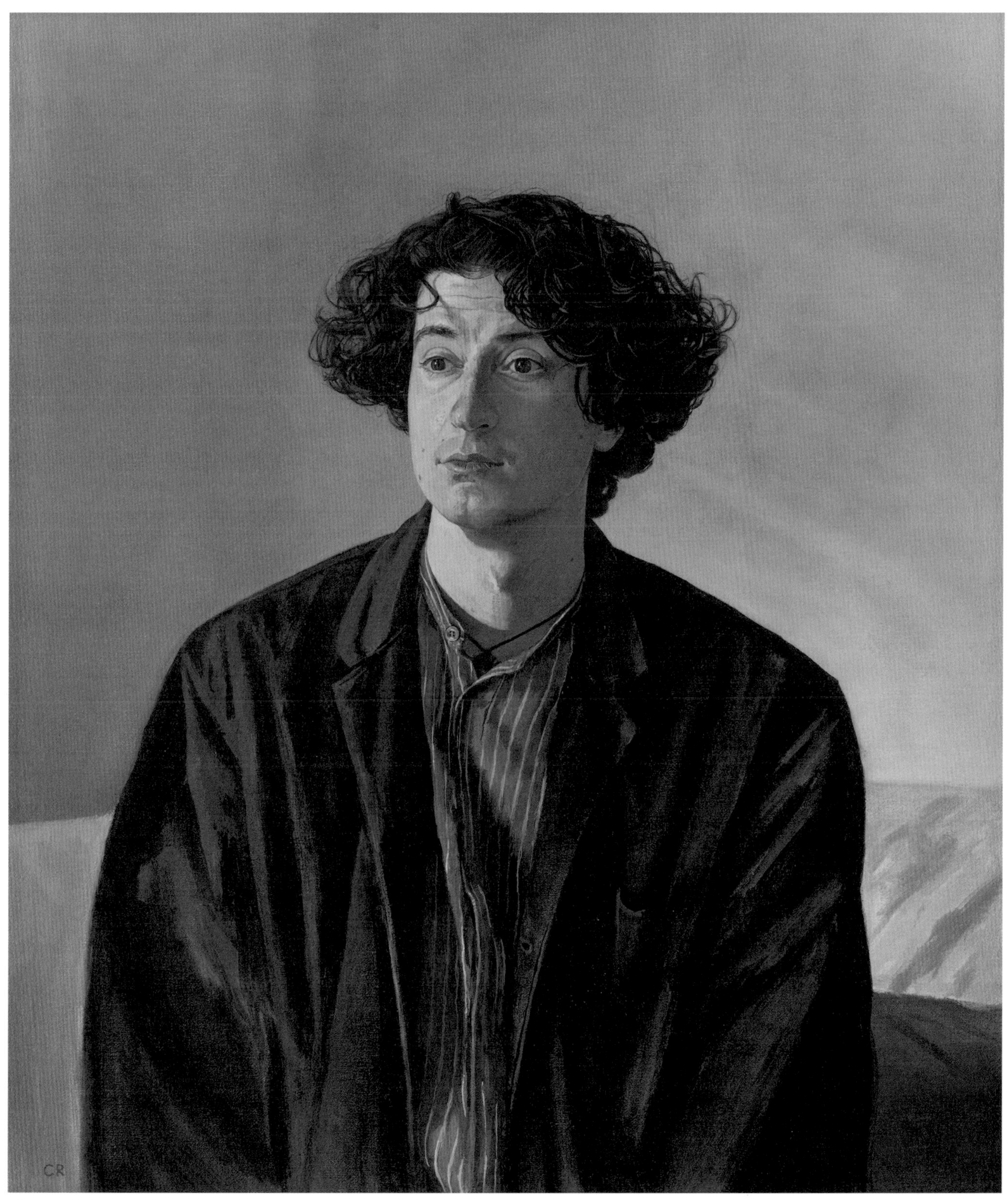

Nathan Ford
*Monument 3*, 2024
Oil on board
740 × 582mm

Based on sittings from more than decade earlier, Nathan Ford painted *Monument 3* over several years as a way to come to terms with his father's death. The artist describes how this posthumous portrait was an 'attempt at solidifying my memories'. The detailed features of his father's eyes and nose are partially obscured and contrast with the limited palette and sparsely painted figure. This gives the impression of his father – and his son's memory of him – gradually receding.

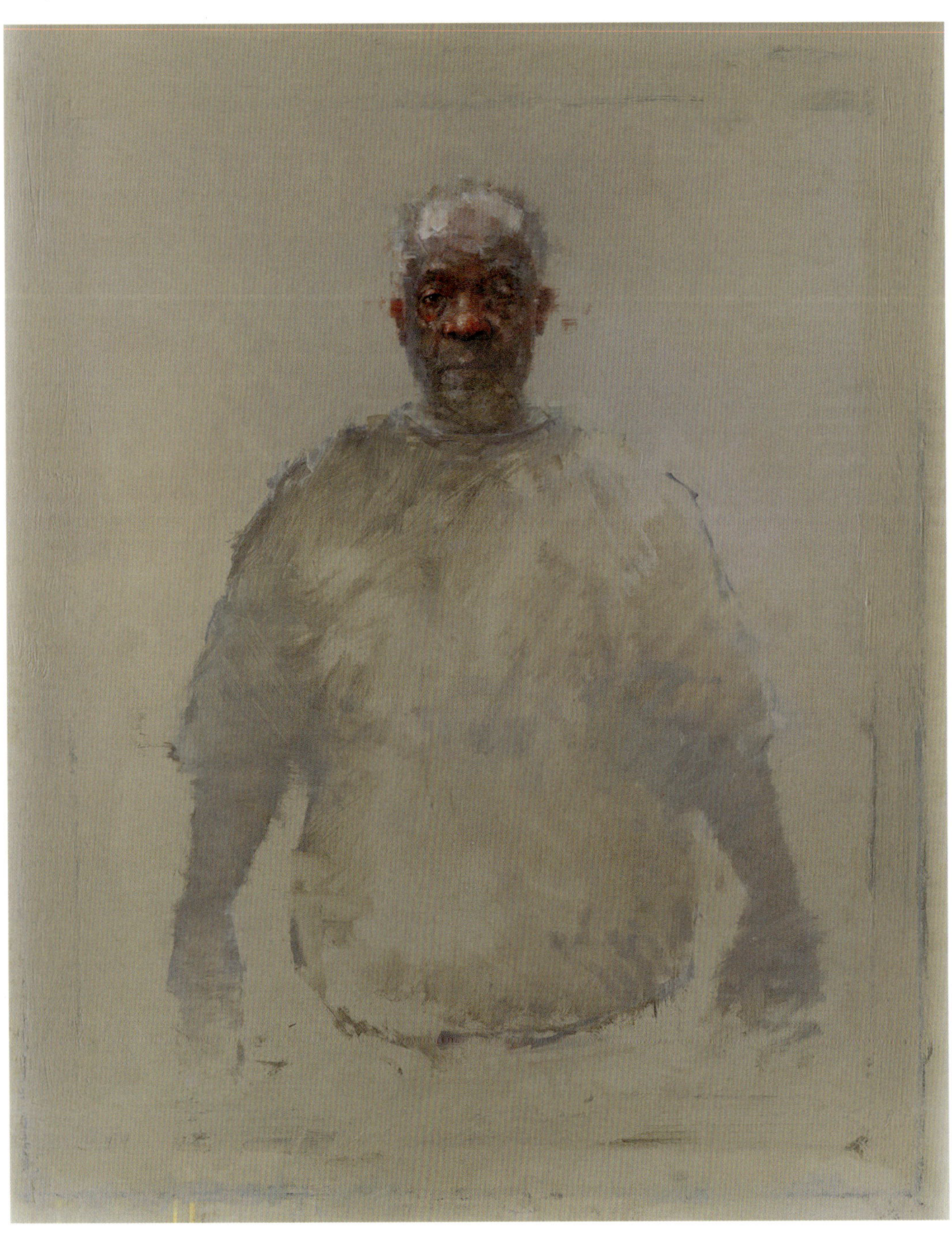

Ruth Fitton
*Onward: Self-Portrait from Life*, 2023
Oil on canvas
1000 × 650mm

With a confident stance, Ruth Fitton proudly asserts
her identity as an artist. She made this self-portrait to
celebrate her tenth anniversary as a self-taught painter.
Working only from life, Fitton used a tilted mirror to create
the complex high-angled viewpoint. She makes direct
references to her artistic process by including her palette
and brushes, and a small colour study from which she was
able to build up the finished painting.

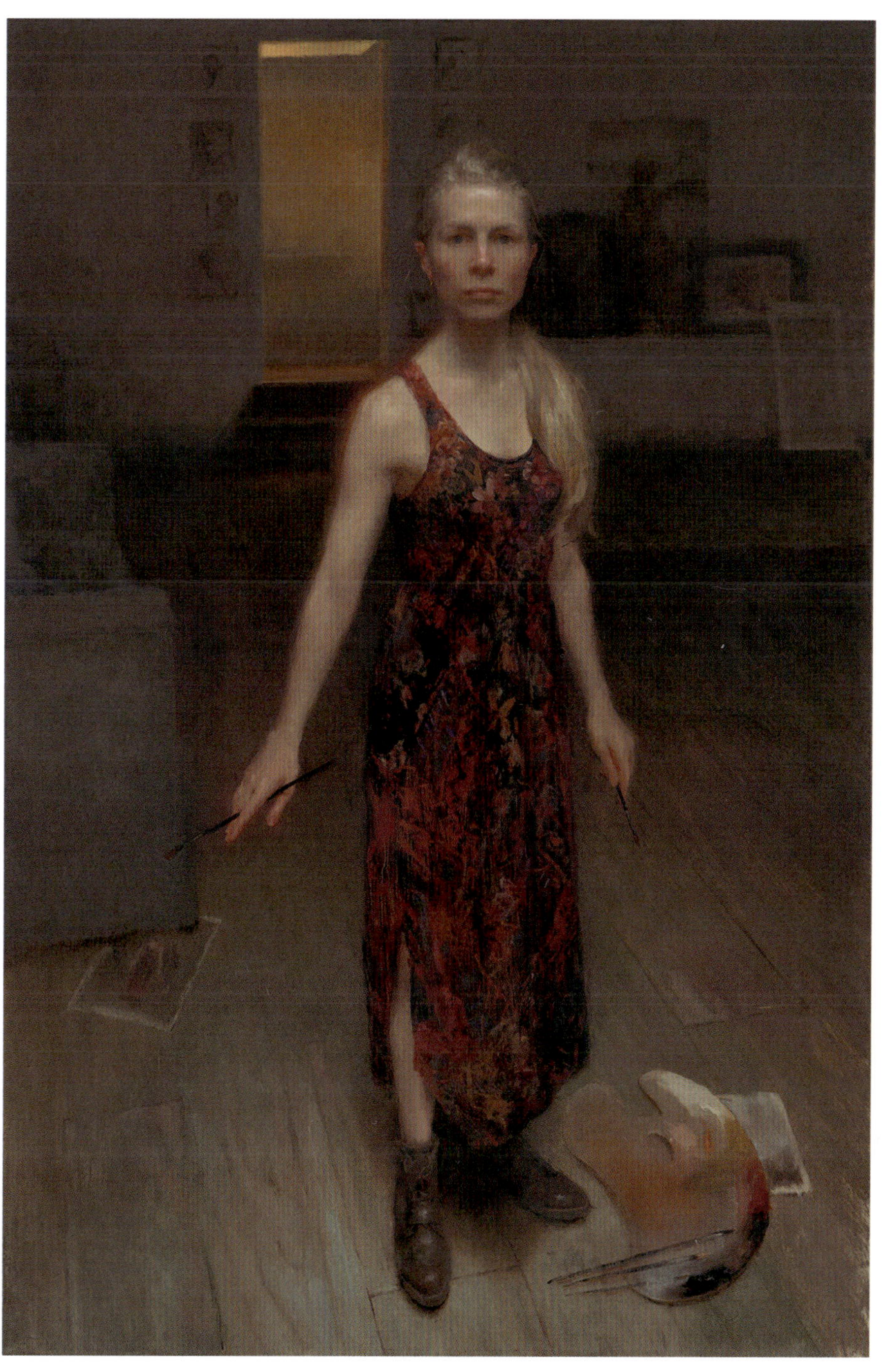

Morag Caister
*Late for school with things on my mind*, 2024
Oil on linen
1204 × 1800mm

*Late for school with things on my mind* is part of Morag Caister's series that depicts different people sitting and lying on her sofa at home. The sitting for this portrait took place over a single day and lasted around six hours, with continual conversation and coffee breaks. After painting the outline of the figure with delicate and repetitious lines, she focused on the colour patches across the skin. Caister seems to have given equal prominence and attention to the plump sofa, painted 'from life', and the sitter, her friend.

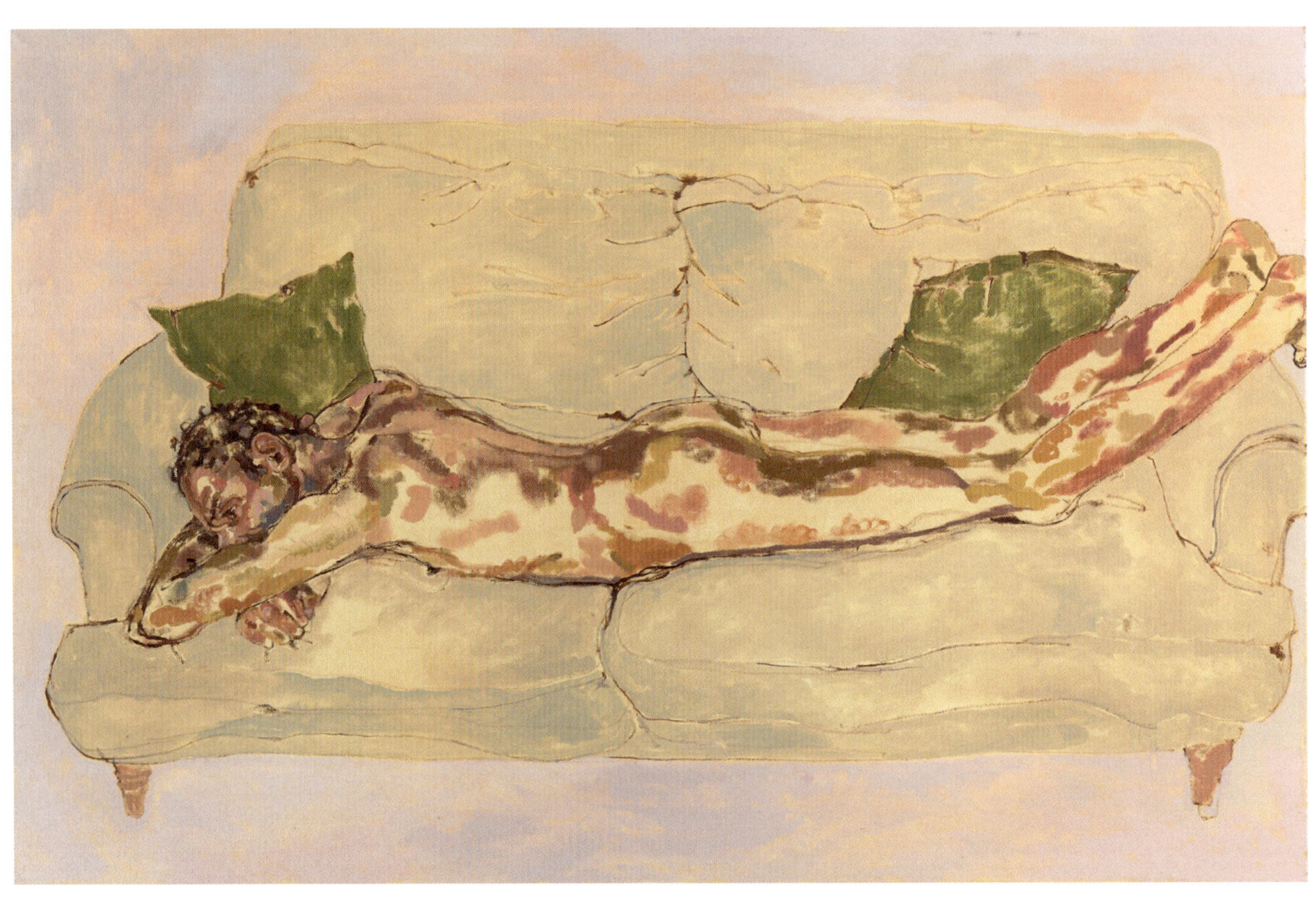

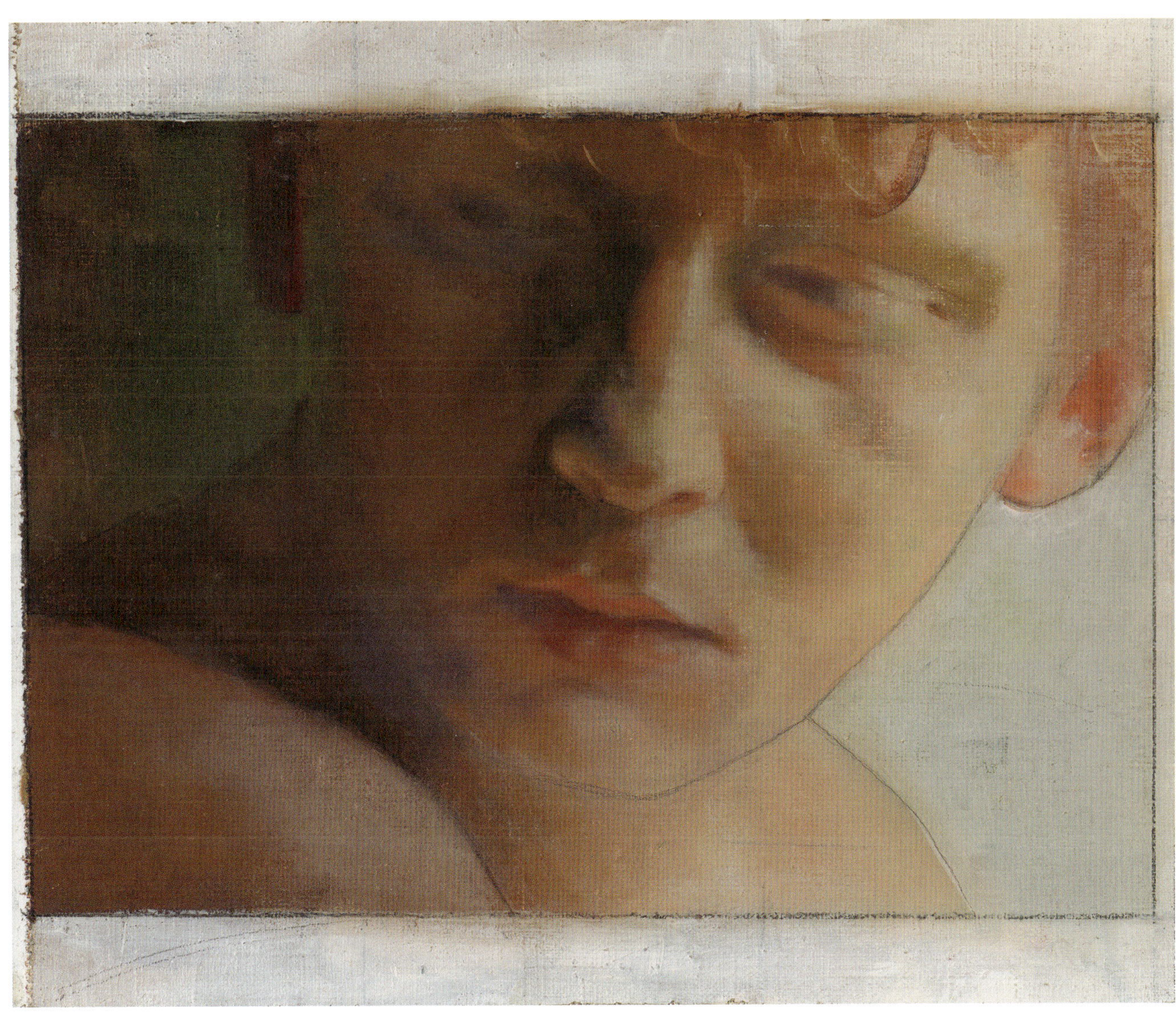

Zohar Tal Inbar
*A Young Man of Light and Gold*, 2023
Oil on canvas
254 × 300mm

Zohar Tal Inbar was struck by the sitter's 'golden colours and lighted soul'. The crude charcoal that surrounds the edges of the painting and the subject's face makes the work appear unfinished or fragmentary. The sitting for this portrait took place just a few weeks before the sitter was kidnapped from his home in Kfar Aza Kibbutz, in southern Israel, and taken hostage during the 7 October 2023 attacks by the armed wing of Hamas. He was later killed by Israeli forces in Gaza after he was mistakenly identified as a threat.

Dan Gaasch
*Selina*, 2022
Oil on canvas
660 × 546mm

Dan Gaasch paints his partner, Selina, in a moment of quiet
repose. The composition and muted colour palette in the
background of the painting aim to draw the viewer's eye
towards Selina's vivid face and striped t-shirt. The artist
is a painting conservator by training, which may have
influenced his decision to leave traces of the painting
process on the canvas such as visible priming, brushstrokes
and an uneven painting surface.

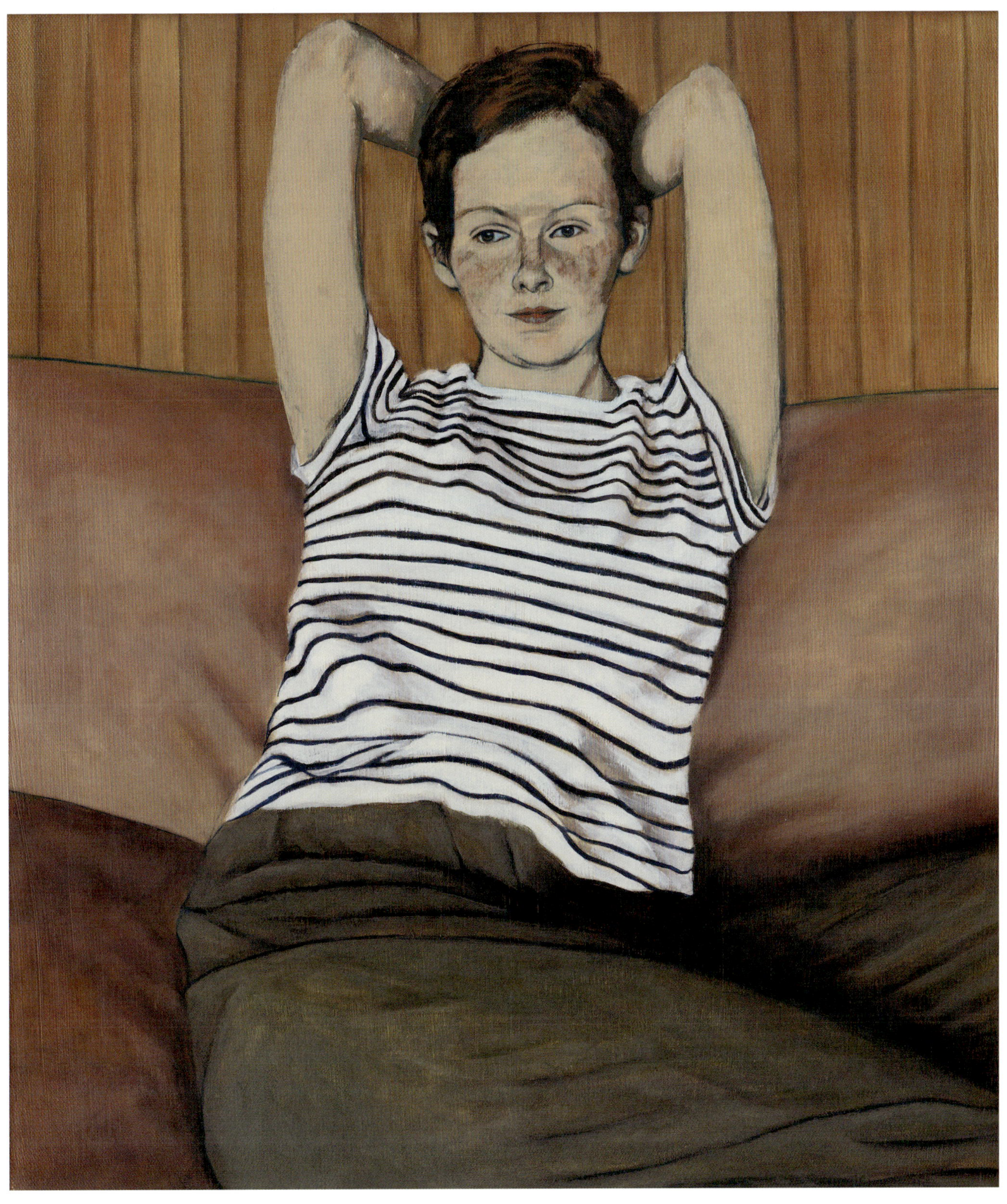

Aleksandra Sokolova
*The Last Portrait*, 2020
Oil on canvas
800 × 1100mm

This portrait is of artist Aleksandra Sokolova's grandfather who was also an artist, as well as a Second World War veteran. He holds a tender and warm expression as he looks out towards his grandchild. As a frequent model, he would often offer guidance as an art mentor during portrait sittings. This work has extra poignancy, as her grandfather died, aged 94, whilst Sokolova was finishing the piece. After making preliminary sketches to define the composition, she used a slow drying technique called 'fat over lean' to apply successive layers of paint, each thicker than the last to ensure a greater colour saturation.

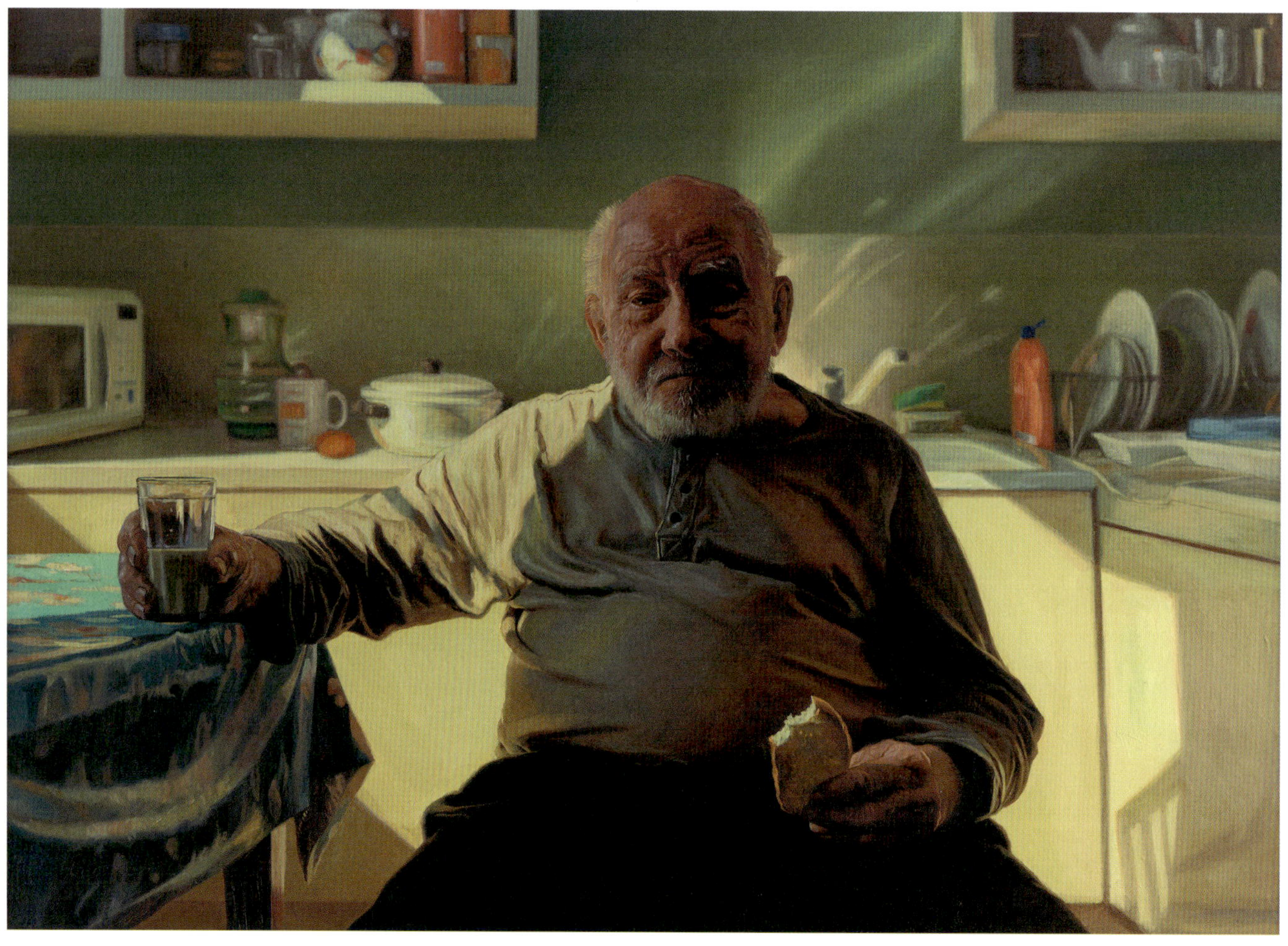

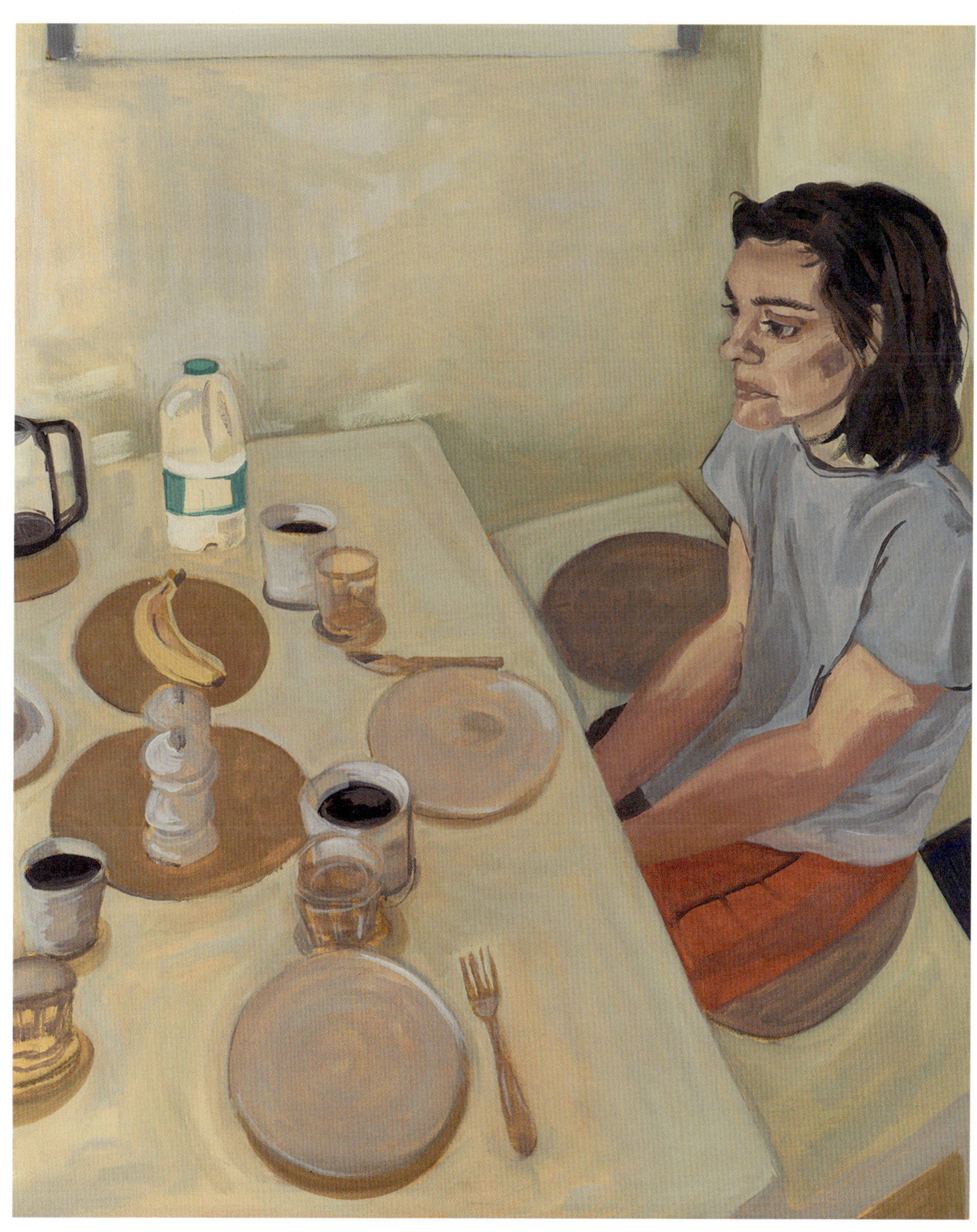

Jane Brodie
*Breakfast with Banana*, 2023
Oil on canvas
760 × 610mm

*Breakfast with Banana* captures the artist, Jane Brodie, and her best friend, Phil, sharing breakfast. Despite usually cherishing this time together to eat and talk, in this moment, Phil was distracted and pensive. The painting is partly informed by memories and photographs of a previous trip spent together when Phil was at a transitional point in her life. The artist's presence is felt through the additional tableware and full coffee cup.

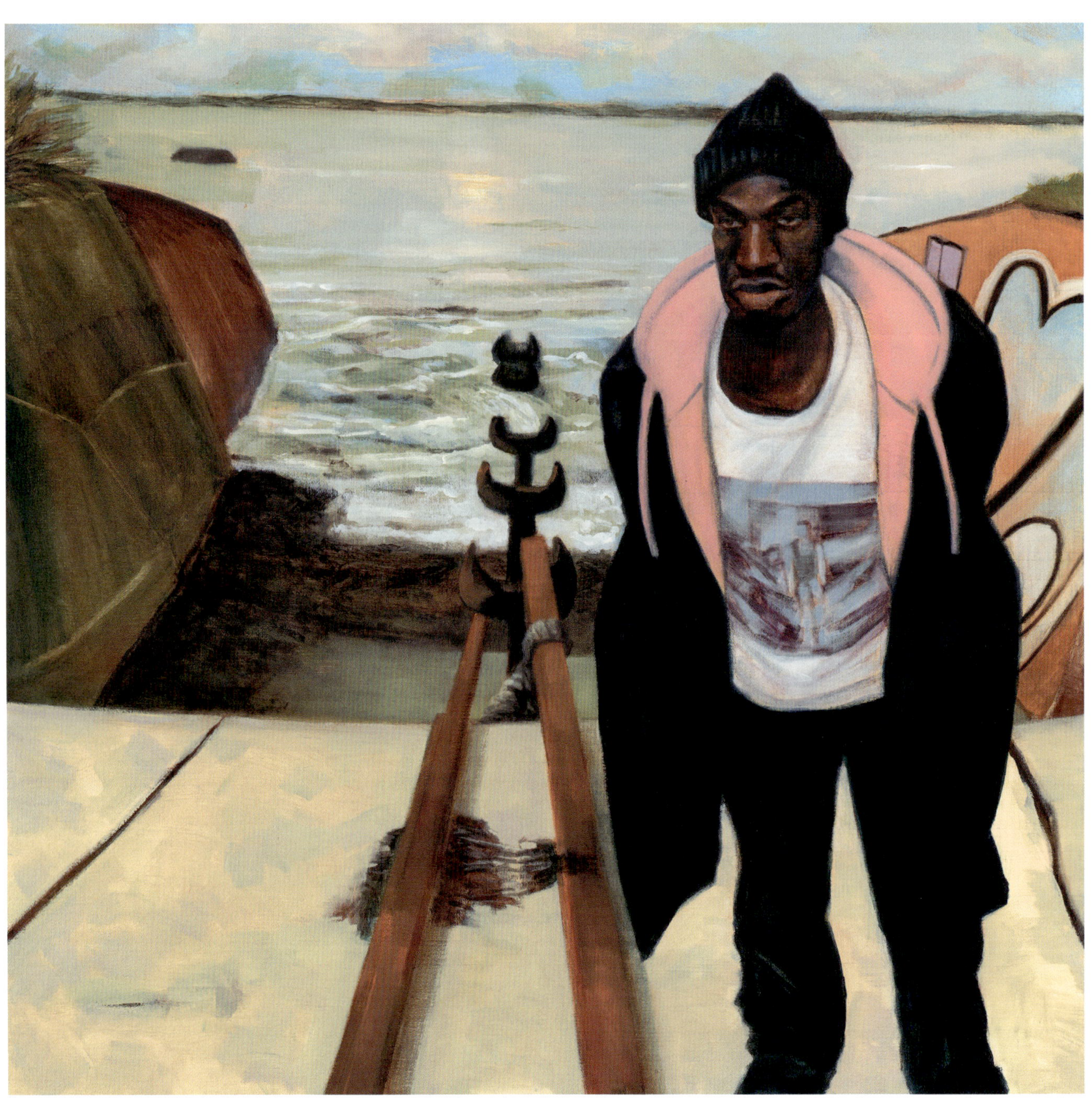

Ray Richardson
*Estuary English*, 2023
Oil on linen
1010 × 1010mm

The sitter, Adé, is a young actor who Ray Richardson met by chance and they felt an instant rapport. The artist explains that they are both from 'working class backgrounds but were working in not very working class games i.e. acting for him and painting for me.' The title refers both to the body of water in the background of the painting and a term used to describe an English accent associated with areas along the River Thames, including London, where both Adé and Richardson live.

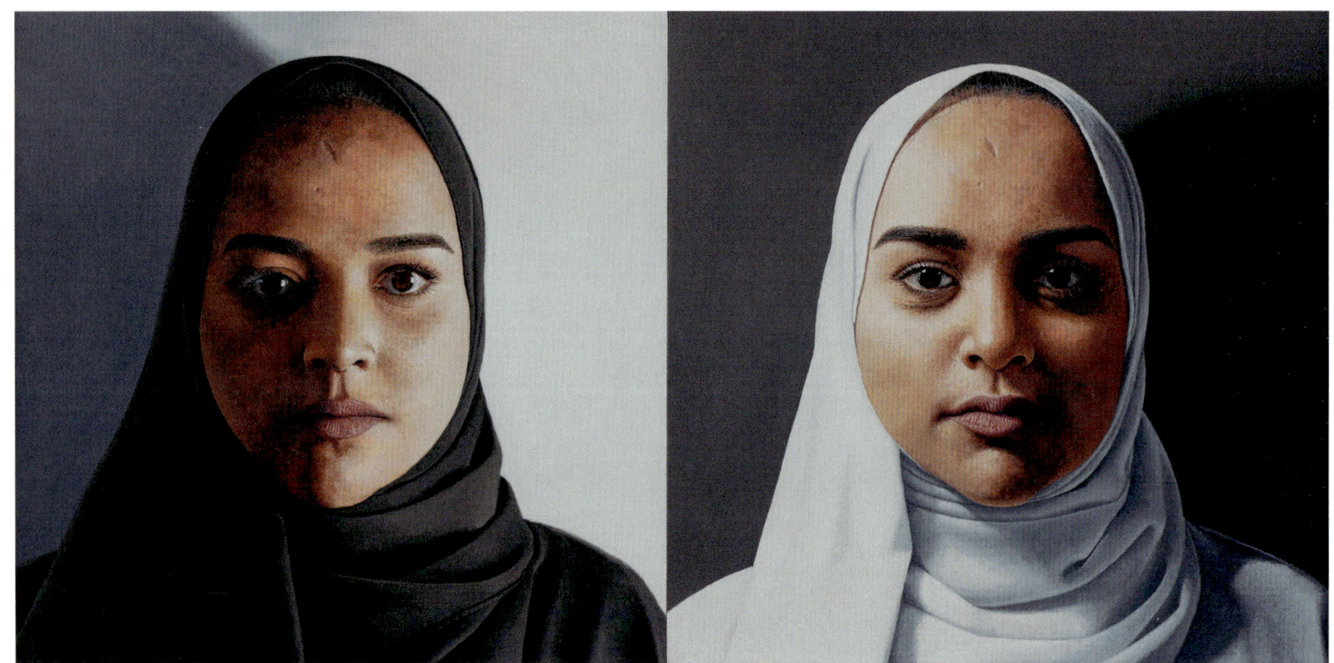

Peter Davis
*Stereo (diptych)*, 2023
Acrylic on canvas
400 × 800mm

Peter Davis wanted to 'explore the viewer's unconscious bias to two juxtaposed portraits of the same Muslim woman'. The sitter, Fahima, was both daunted and excited by the prospect of sitting for this portrait. After seeing the finished work, she was intrigued by how 'different coloured hijabs make me look different, something I'd never particularly thought about before.' The artist referenced hundreds of photographs that were taken during one sitting, paying close attention to the use of light and shade to inform the tonal contrasts in the finished painting.

Stephen Leho
*The Most Important Thing in the World*, 2020
Oil on canvas
540 × 480mm

*The Most Important Thing in the World* depicts Stephen Leho's partner who was emerging from a period of strained mental health. Thread by thread, she is shown untangling a homemade mobile made from foil and string. The artist explains how 'the tangled mobile reflects the turmoil of her universe ... turned away and oblivious to the viewer, she is determined to pacify her world'.

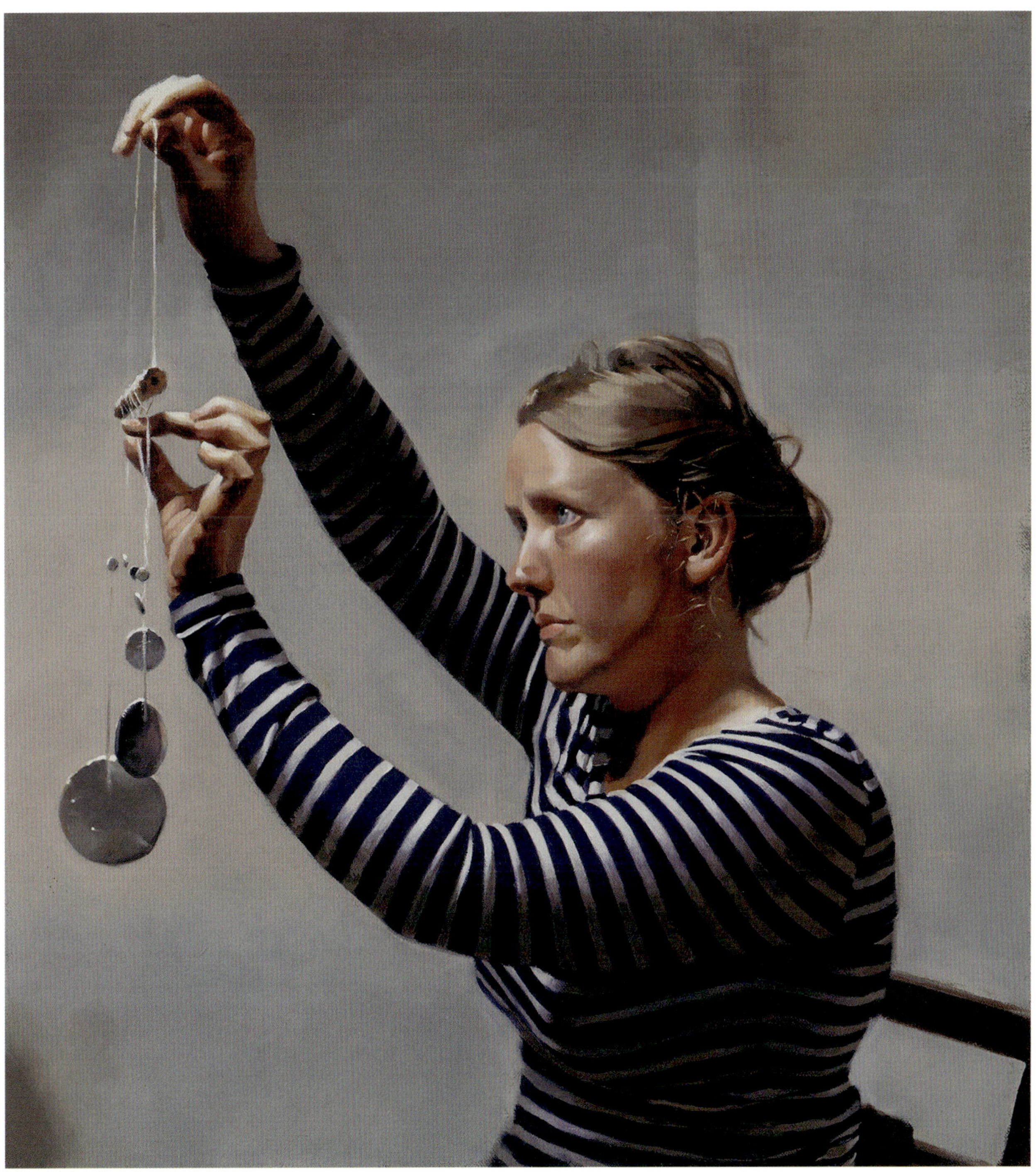

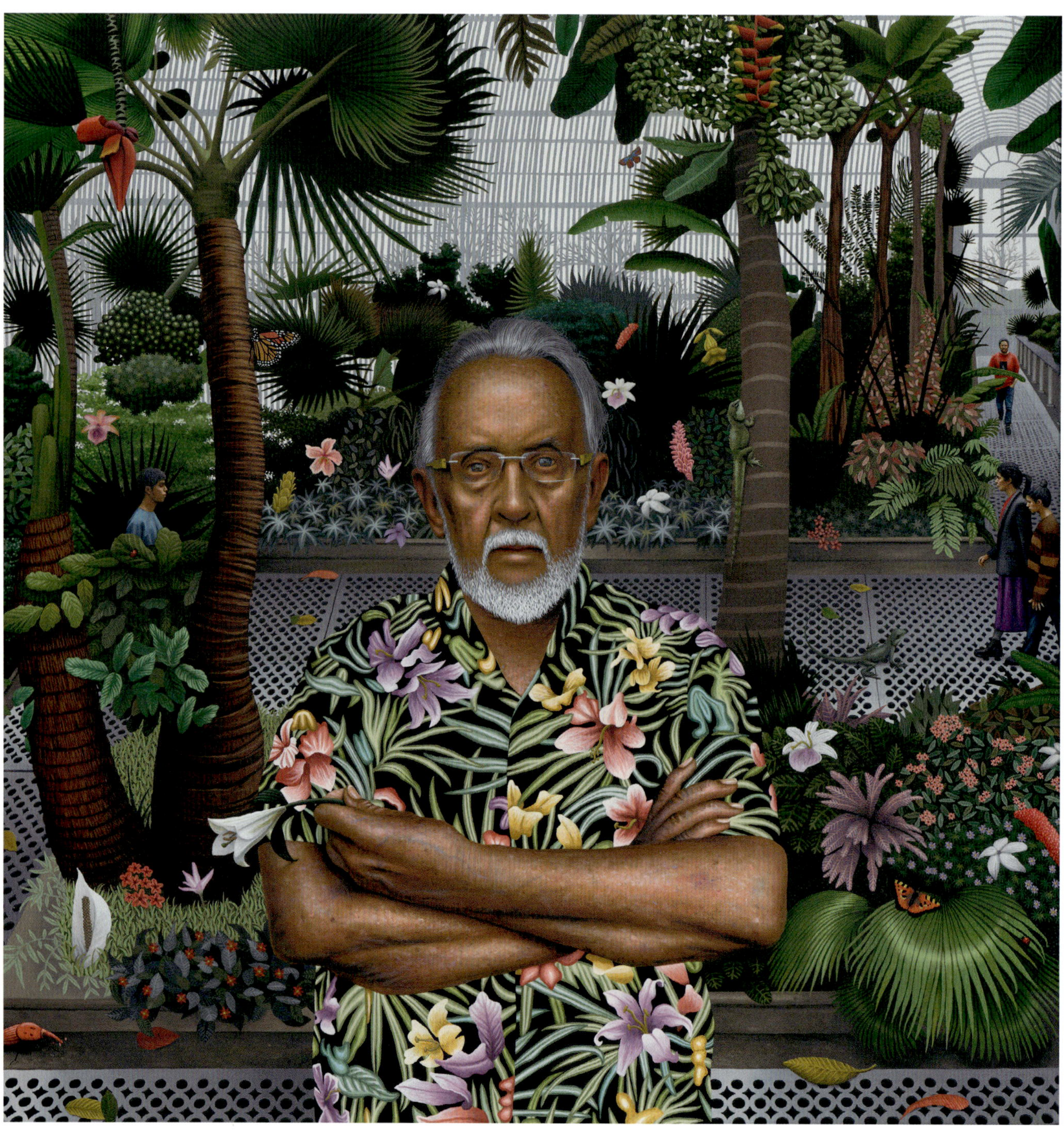

Carl Randall
*Alain at Kew*, 2022
Oil on canvas
750 × 710mm

Carl Randall depicts Alain in front of the Palm House,
a Victorian greenhouse in Kew Gardens, London.
Whilst making the work, Randall would visit the National
Gallery in London to study the detailed paintings of
Early Netherlandish artists, such as Jan van Eyck and
Rogier van der Weyden. Using the Old Master Verdaccio
technique, the artist applied semi-translucent layers
of skin-coloured tones on top of green underpainting.
The blemishes and wrinkles on the sitter's skin, and
the wilting Iris flower, contrast with Kew's blossoming
flora. The family featured in the background of the work
commissioned the portrait.

Shinji Ihara
*1111*, 2023
Oil on canvas
728 × 910mm

Japanese artist, Shinji Ihara, records his partner on the day their beloved cat passed away. It took Ihara almost a year, and over 90 sittings, to complete this intricate portrait. During the sittings, he would be reminded of that fateful day and try to capture in oil 'everything I felt at that time'. The detritus of their shared lives surrounds his partner; the unmade bunk beds and two coffee cups signal the artist's presence.

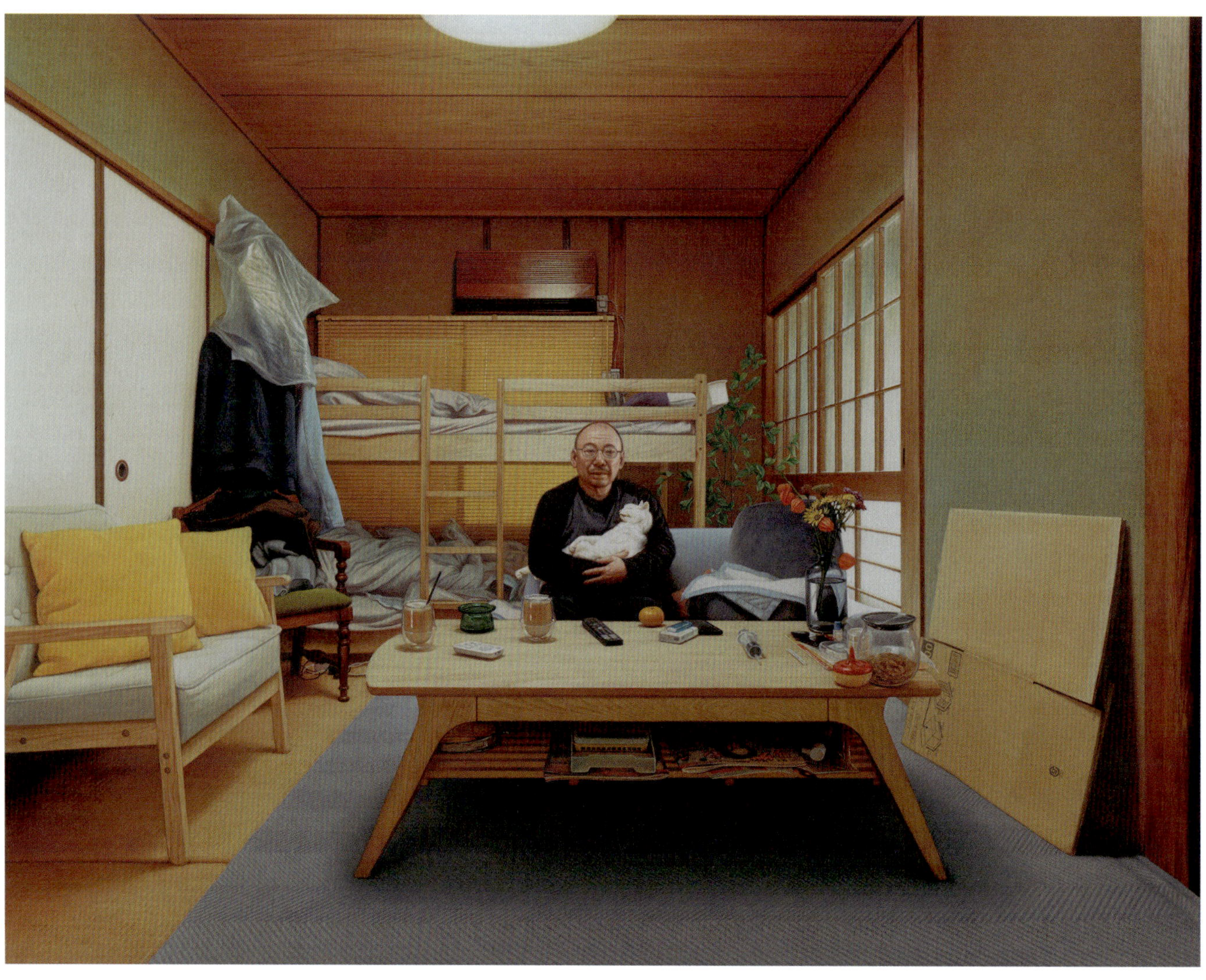

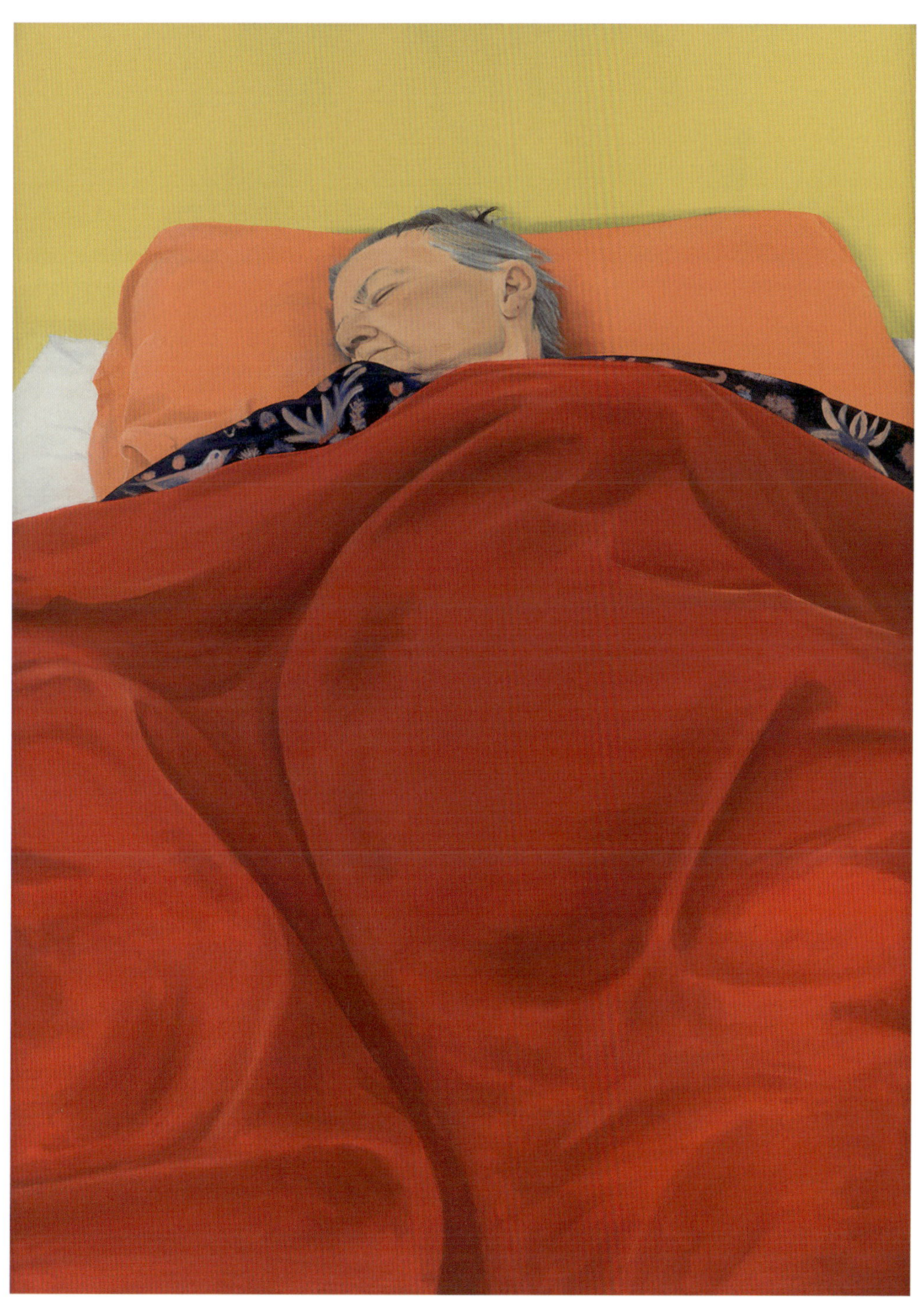

Laura Carey
*I'll Never Not Miss You*, 2023
Oil on canvas
700 × 500mm

Laura Carey painted her mother enveloped in a bright red blanket during an afternoon sleep brought on by her chemotherapy treatment. She explains: 'Her blanket is my love, my anger, hopelessness, grief as well as her cancer all at once.' Whilst the making of the work was emotionally painful, it was also cathartic, a way for the artist 'to face grief head-on, and challenge the taboo of dying and death.'

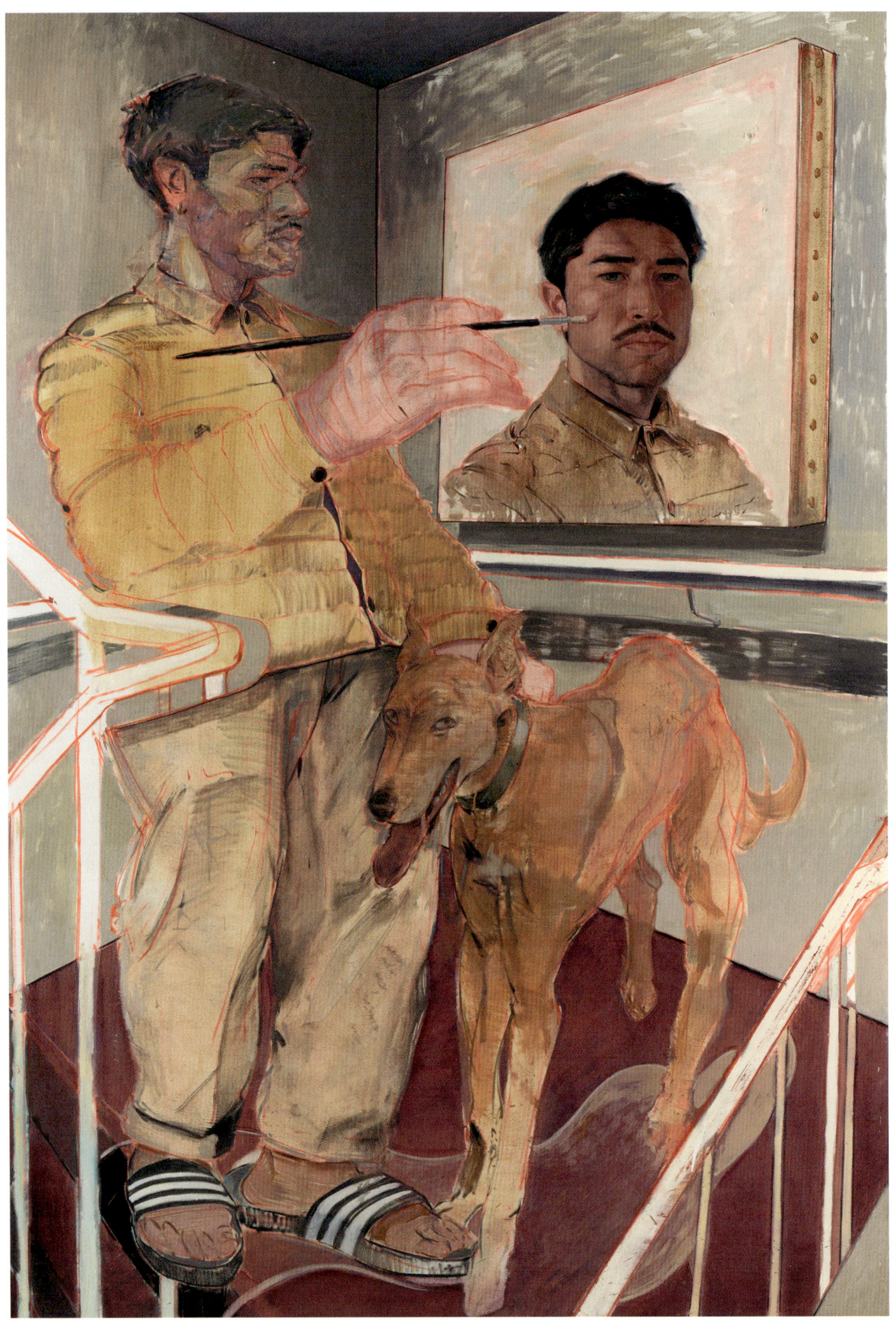

Shane Keisuke Berkery
*A Self-Portrait*, 2024
Oil on canvas
2400 × 1600mm

In this intriguing self-portrait, the Irish-Japanese painter,
Shane Keisuke Berkery, presents a towering, stylised
version of himself in the process of painting a more
realistic and traditional head and shoulders self-portrait.
The setting is the stairwell of the Royal College of Art,
London, where Berkery studied for his MA in Painting.
The concept of the double self-portrait emerged following
a traumatic event involving his dog, Milo, also depicted,
to convey how 'our outward presentation of ourselves
seldom accurately reflects our internal world.'

Emily Stainer
*Frederick*, 2023
Oil on canvas
300mm (diameter)

In this portrait, Emily Stainer portrays her son, Frederick,
having just returned home from a school cricket match.
Flushed and tired, yet also exhilarated, the artist captures
this moment of youthful exuberance. The format of the
small round painting references Elizabethan portrait
miniatures, connecting a contemporary subject to a
personal and intimate historic portrait tradition.

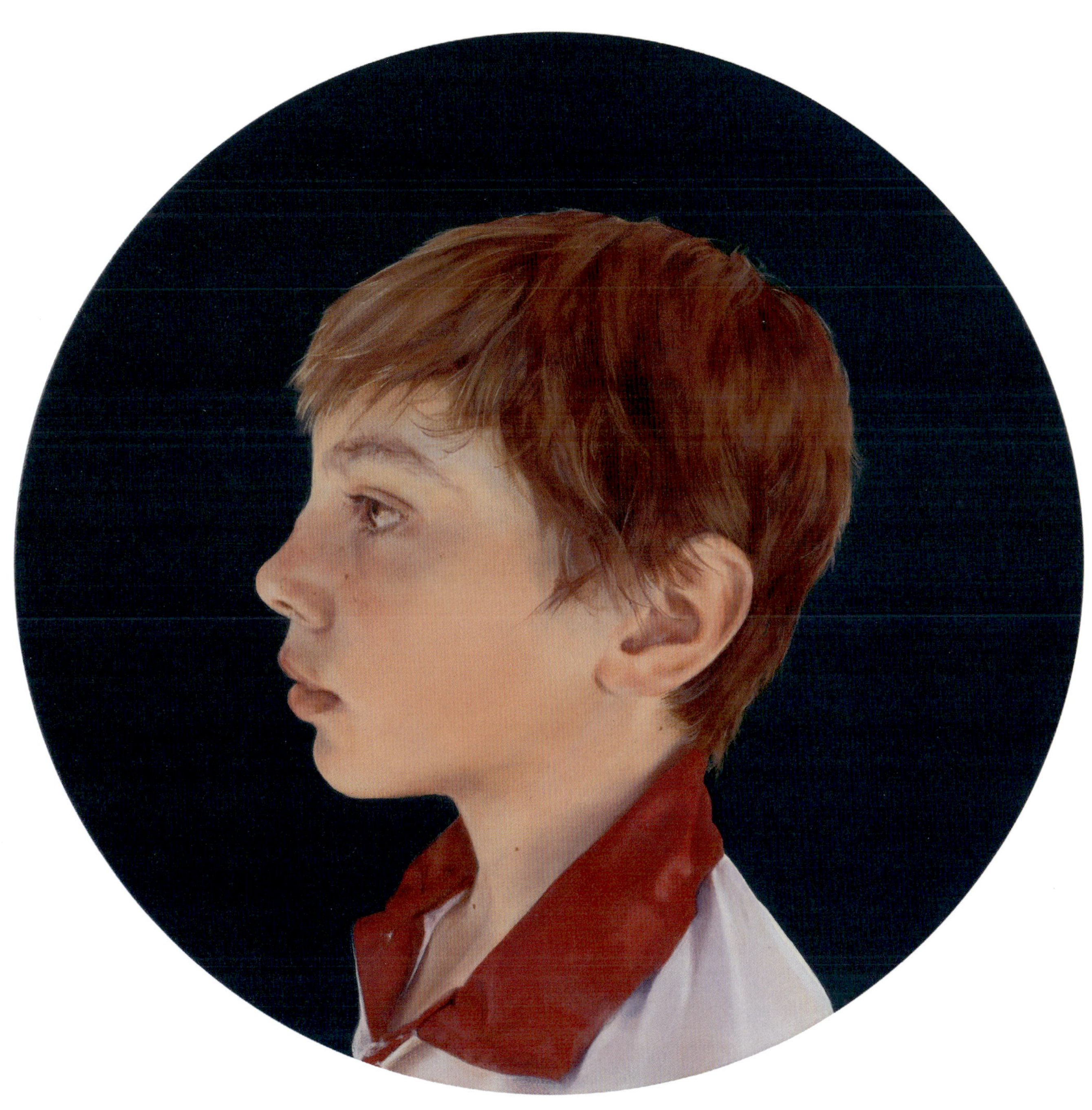

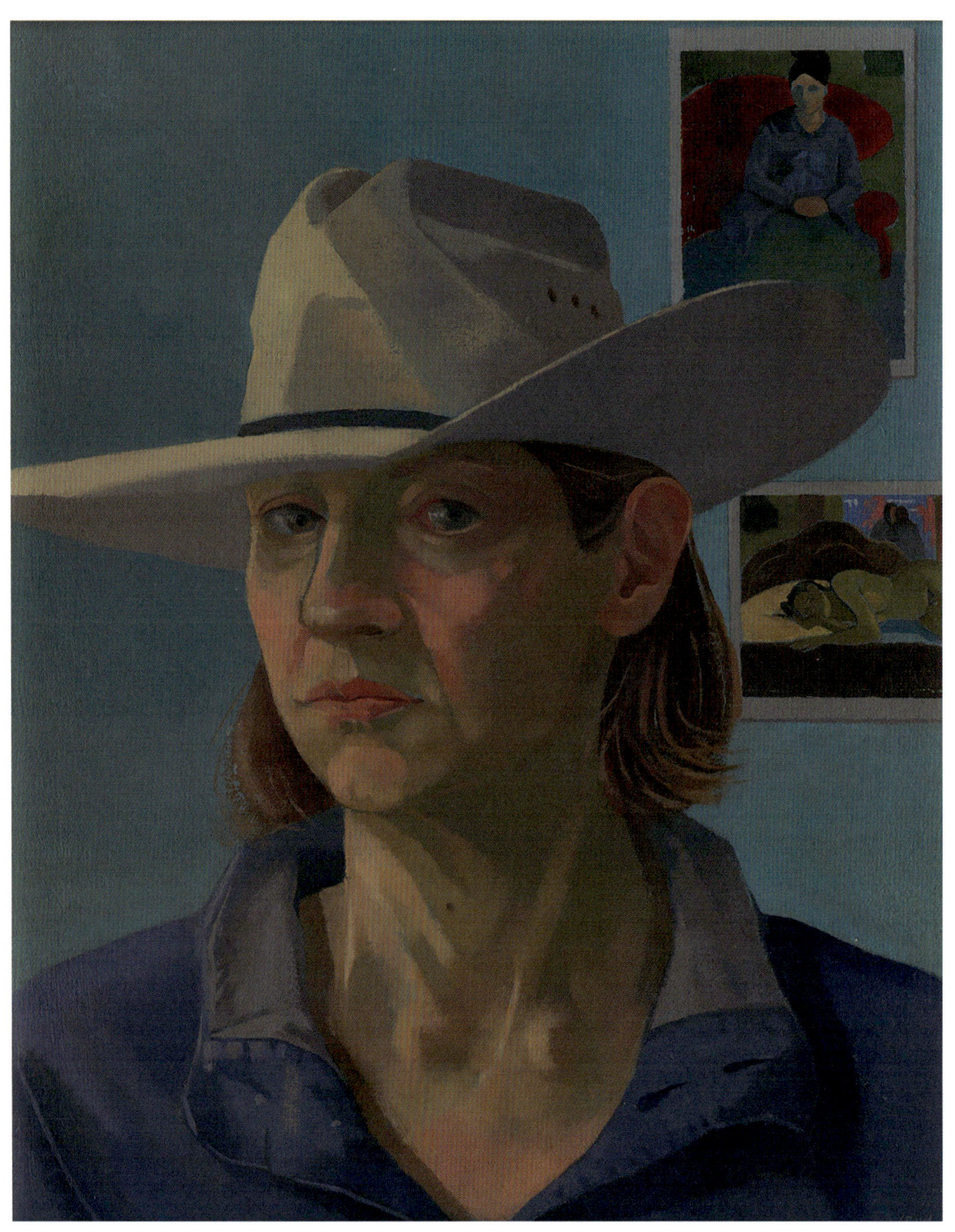

Caroline Bays
*Reflection with Postcards*, 2021
Oil on board
510 × 410mm

Caroline Bays created this self-portrait at the height of the Covid-19 pandemic. It was painted from direct observation in daylight using a mirror. The artist was interested in exploring the effects of light and contrast on her face. Postcards stuck to the wall behind Bays hint at her artistic influences, *Madame Cézanne in a Red Armchair* by Paul Cézanne (*c.*1877) and *Nevermore* by Paul Gauguin (1897).

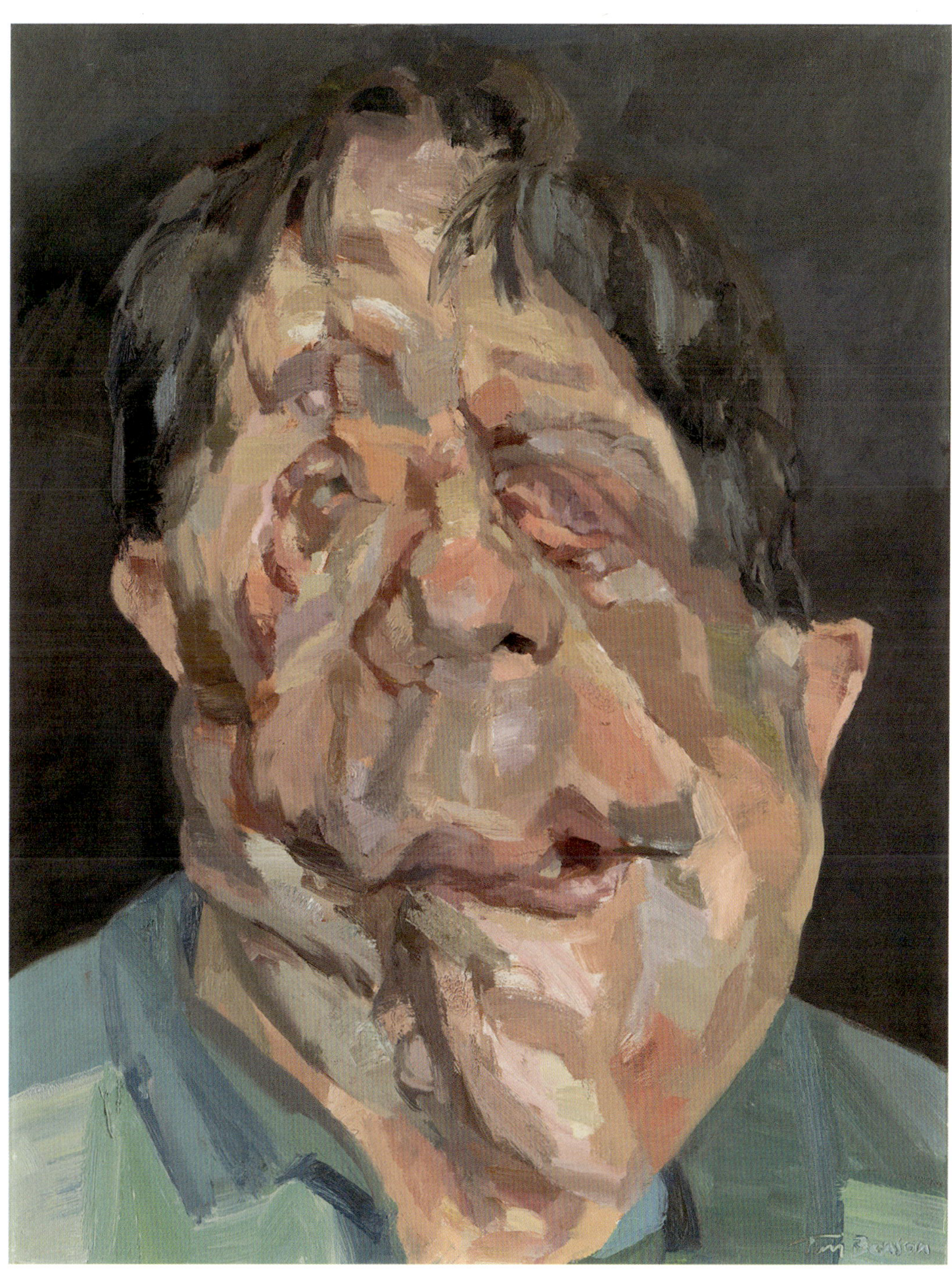

Tim Benson
*Adam Pearson*, 2023
Oil on canvas
1220 × 910mm

Tim Benson depicts the British actor, TV presenter and disability rights campaigner, Adam Pearson. Pearson has neurofibromatosis, a condition that causes benign tumours to grow on and under his skin. During the sitting, Pearson felt 'respected and comfortable and therefore instantly trusted Tim's motivations.' The larger than life scale encourages the viewer to confront the stigma often associated with facial disfigurements.

Jack Freeman
*Anna*, 2023
Oil on canvas
700 × 500mm

Jack Freeman paints his partner Anna resting with an
empty cup of tea. Preferring to depict those closest
to him, here the artist captures a scene of domestic
intimacy. He introduces different textural elements to
the composition including the thickly knitted jumper,
which contrasts with the delicately painted strands
of hair that form a halo-like effect as they spread out
towards the painting's edges. The portrait took several
months to complete and was made using a combination
of photographic studies and sittings from life.

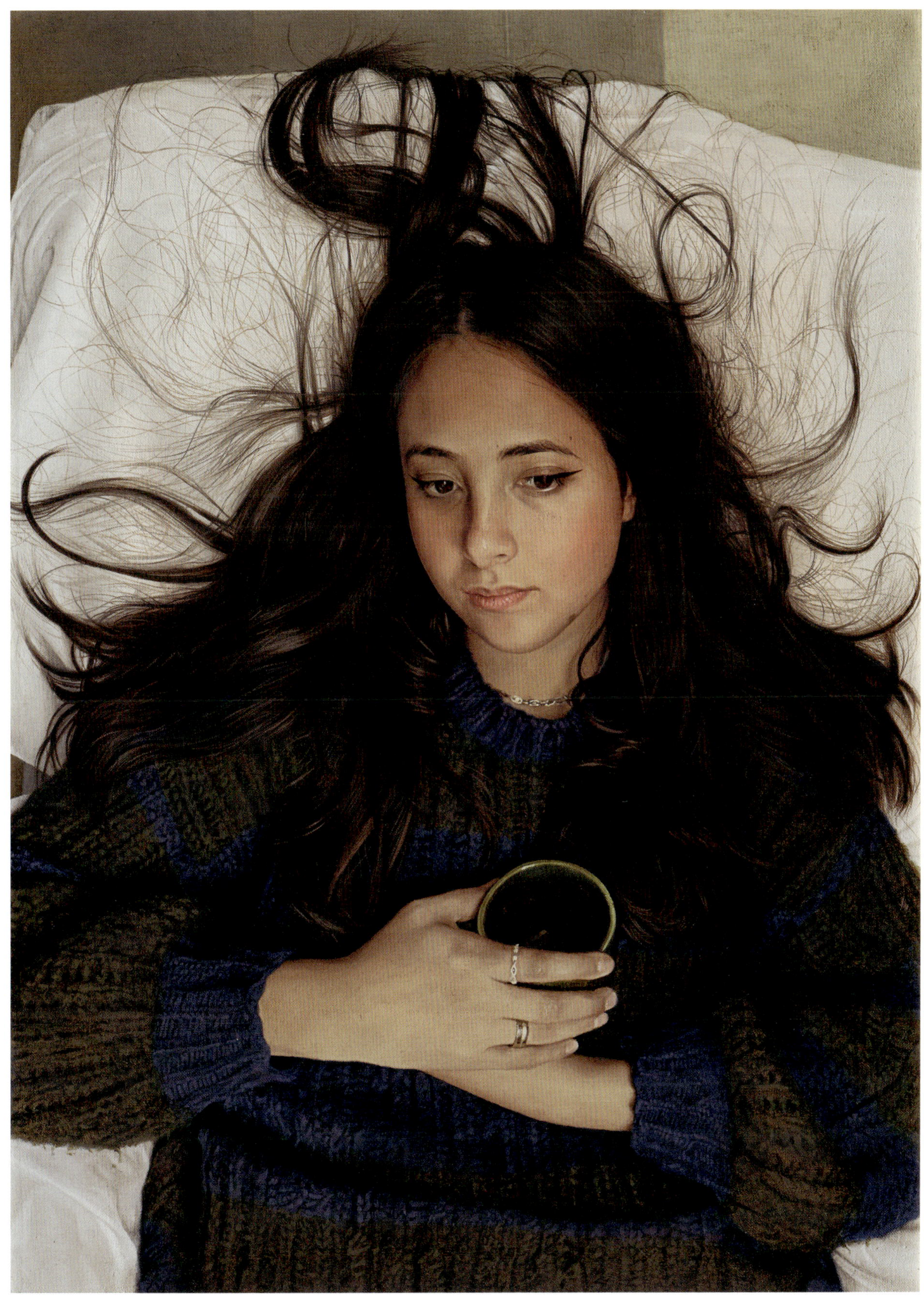

Dawn Beckles
*A Moment*, 2024
Acrylic, gold leaf and oil on canvas
1200 × 800mm

*A Moment* is a vibrant self-portrait that captures a fleeting moment of happiness whilst in the studio. Dawn Beckles explains that she was attempting to immortalise 'the moments that slip through the cracks of memory and documentation.' The self-taught artist creates colourful mixed-media paintings of still life and interiors, often with exotic flora inspired by her native home, Barbados. The year '1981' emblazoned on her green jumper references the year she was born.

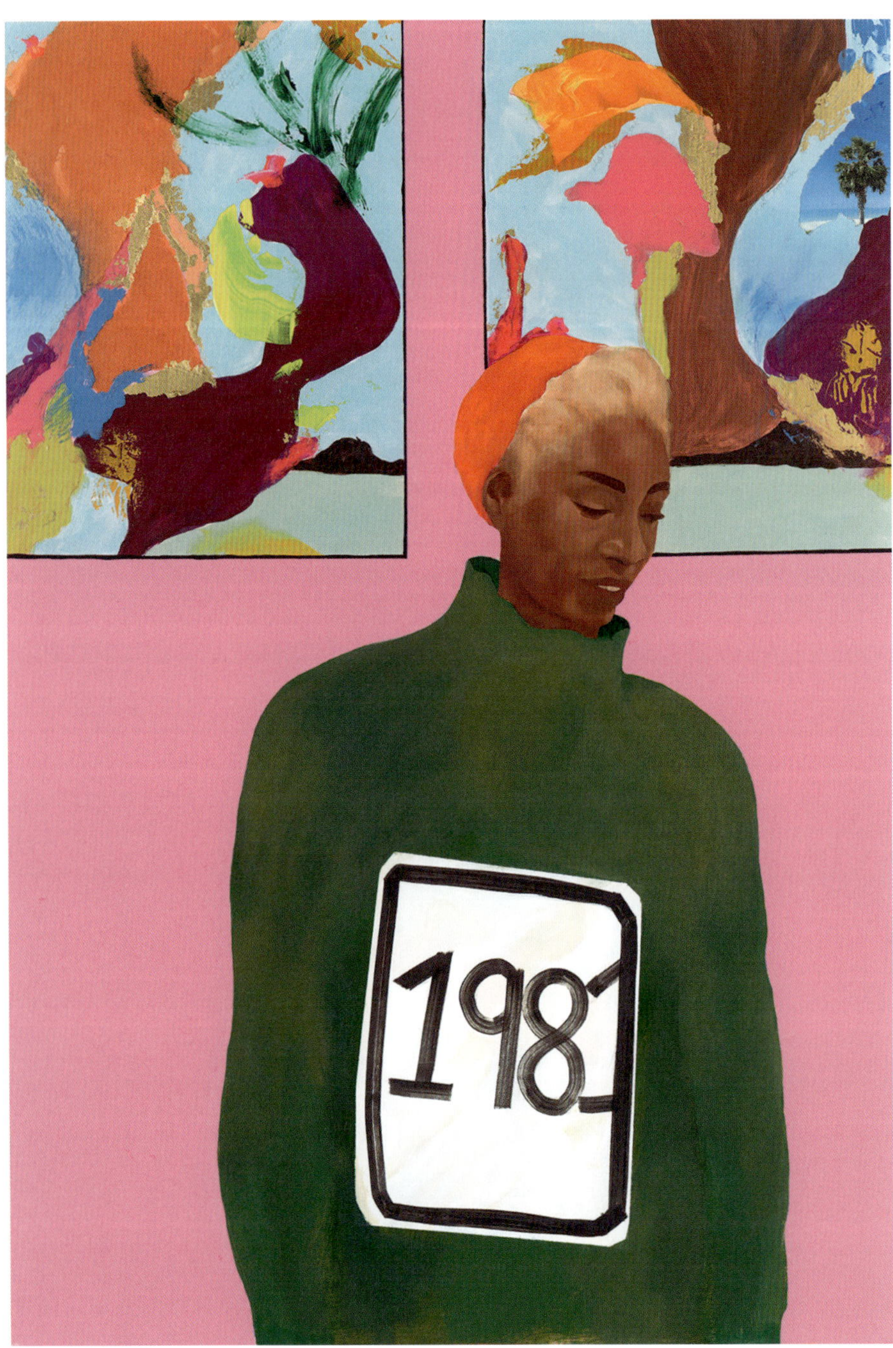

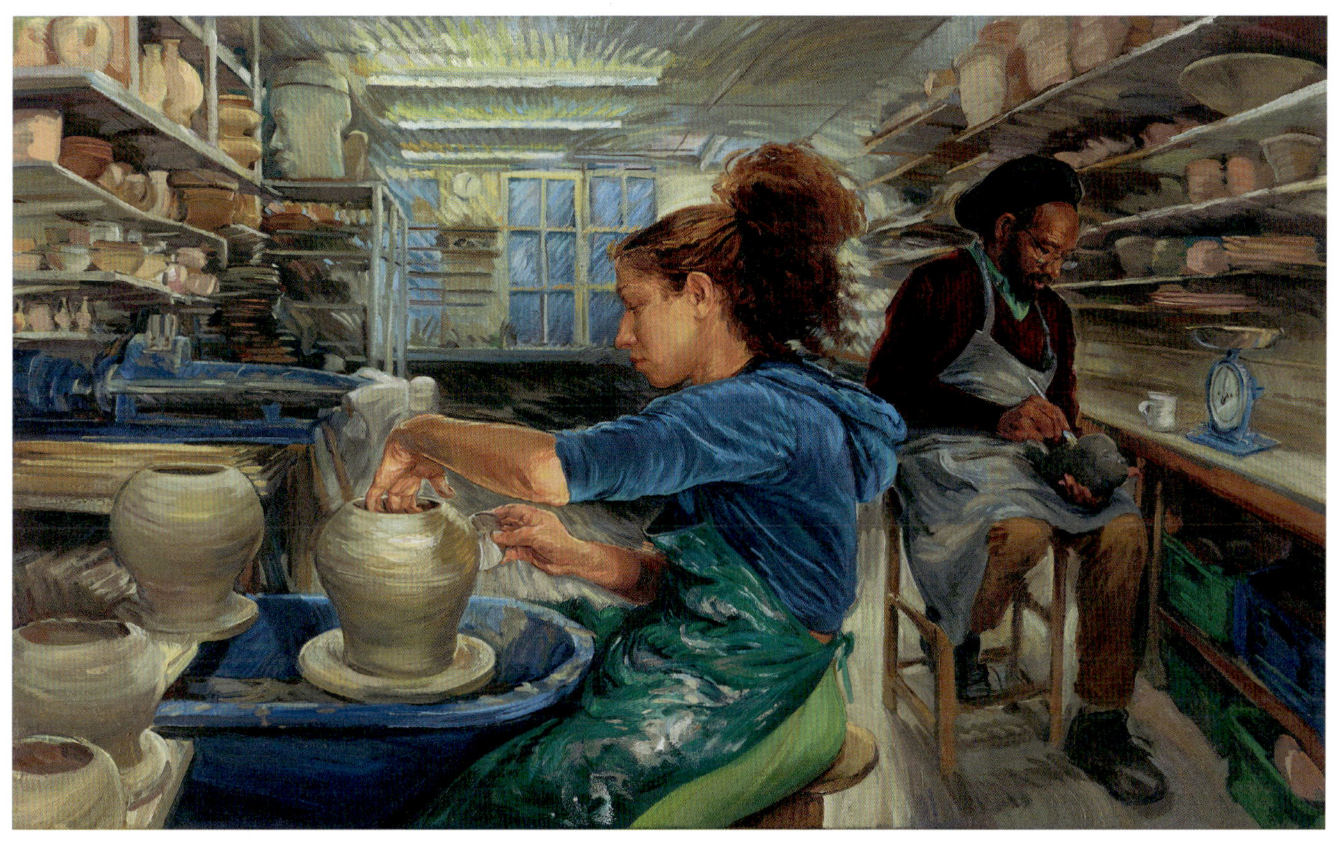

Lewis Hazelwood-Horner
*The Brambles*, 2023
Oil on linen
600 × 1000mm

Lewis Hazelwood-Horner describes their work of two generations of ceramicists as capturing the 'intricate dance of creativity and tradition'. The narrowing perspective and quickly applied marks draw the viewer into the buzz of the studio, and like clay, the painting seems to warp and bend. Although Freya and her father Chris face away from each other, their closeness is implied through the act of working side by side in their shared passion.

Gustavo Schossler
*Ingrid*, 2023
Oil on linen
440 × 510mm

Ingrid is a professional model with albinism. Brazilian
artist, Gustavo Schossler, was drawn to paint her.
Commenting on the importance of representing diverse
people in paintings, Ingrid says: 'beauty comes in
many different forms, all worthy of being painted and
celebrated.' Created from life over several sittings, the
artist explained that there was 'a lot of push and pull,
where I apply paint and remove it, find and lose shapes,
always looking for the right form and passage of colour.'

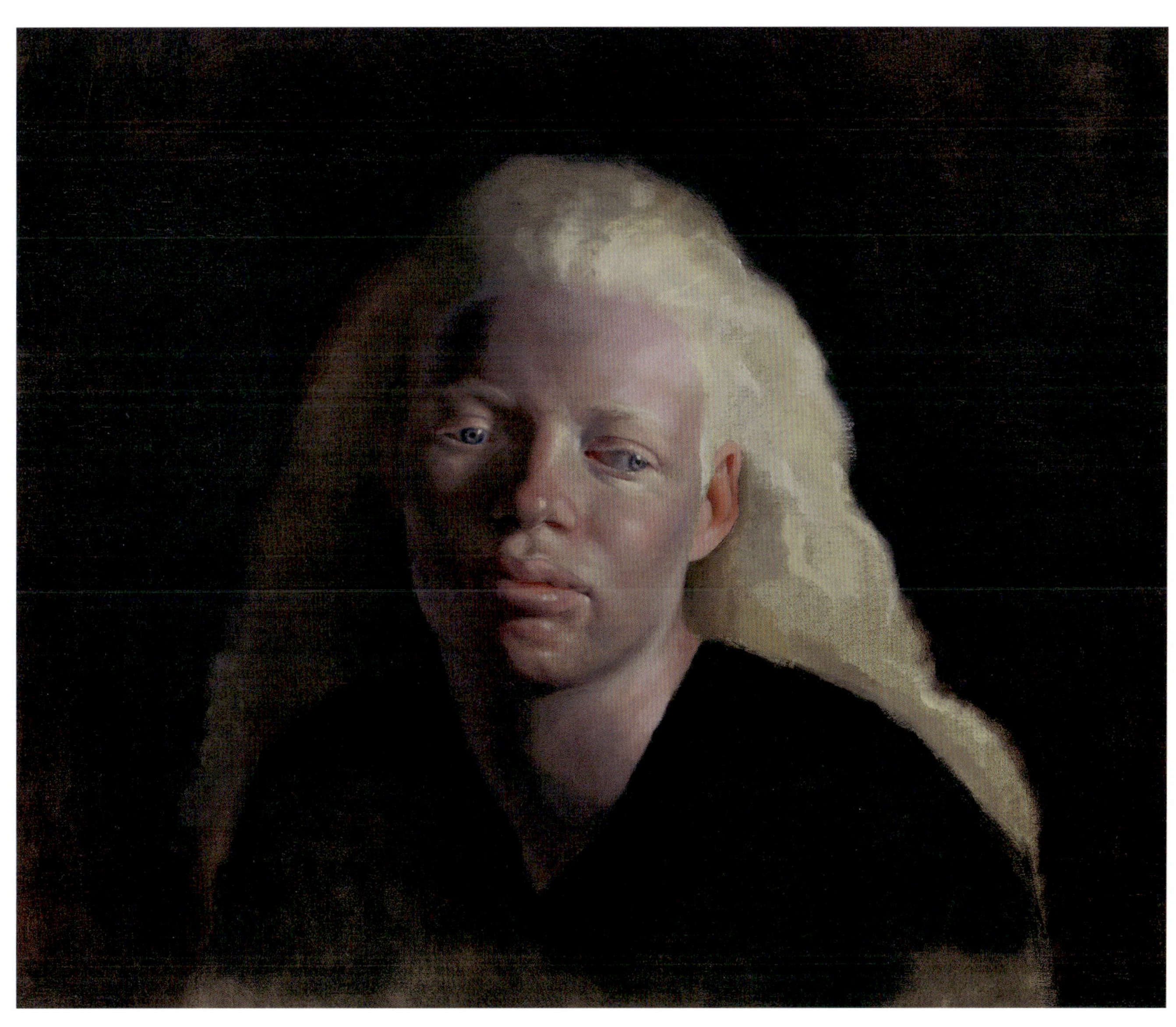

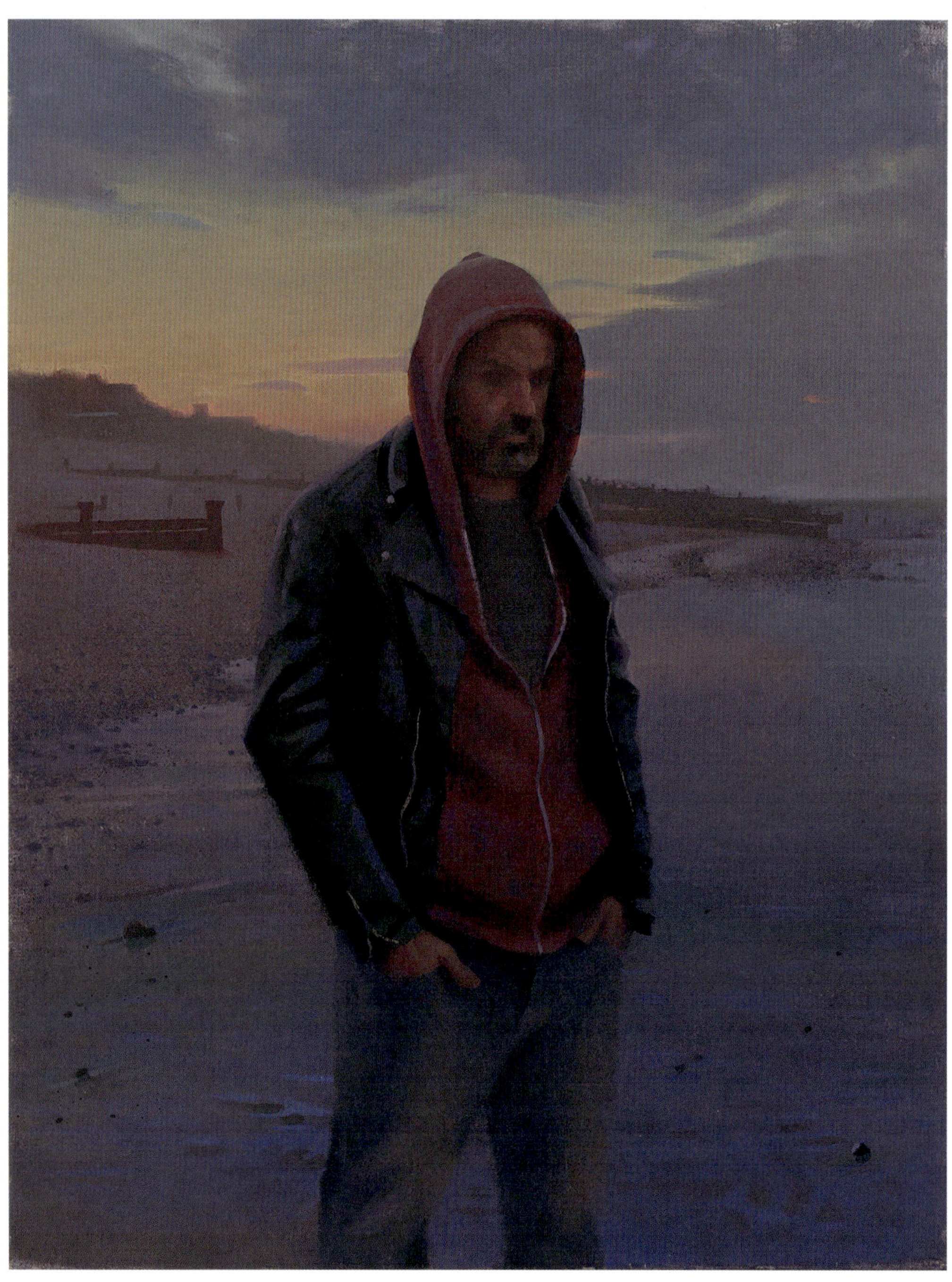

Alex Tzavaras
*Self-Portrait at Low Tide*, 2023
Oil on linen
600 × 450mm

Whist walking on Bexhill-on-Sea beach, Alex Tzavaras became fascinated by the reflections of the sky at sunrise on the wet sand at low tide. The artist was struggling with his mental health and this experience filled him with hope, inspiring this self-portrait. Overcoming the outdoor conditions, he took photographs and produced studies of the landscape with his figure reflected in a mirror. It took several years and multiple attempts before he felt he had successfully captured the effect that initially caught his eye.

Laura Critchlow
*The Artist's Mother*, 2022
Oil on board
500 × 400mm

Laura Critchlow's mother holds an earthworm in reference to how she never walks past a struggling worm without returning it to where they should be. The artist explains how her mother does the same for her: 'She sets me back on track during difficult times. She is a protector.' Critchlow is a self-taught artist who uses traditional oil painting techniques, whereby she applies many layers of paint and glazing to create depth.

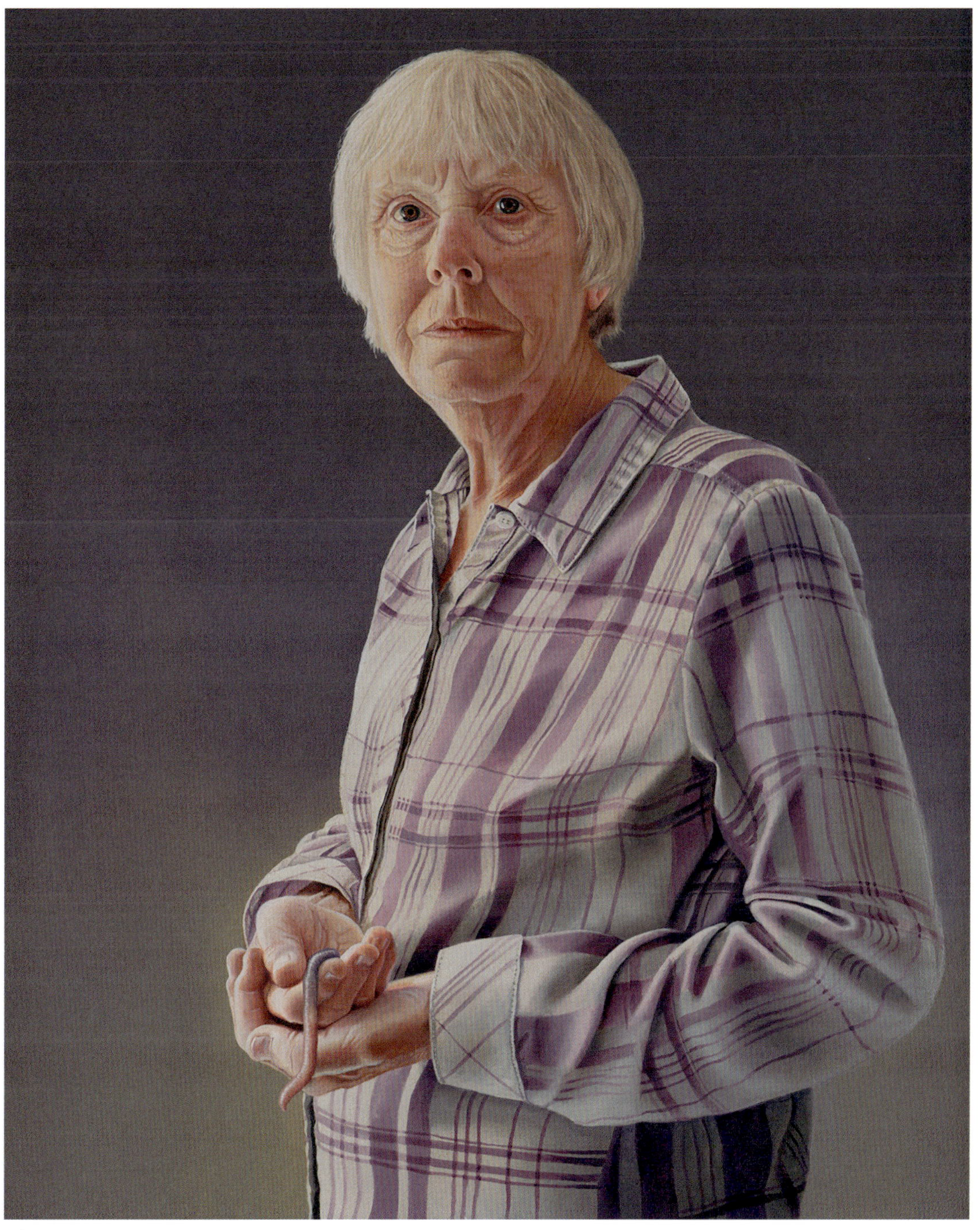

Stephen Johnston
*Francis*, 2024
Oil on linen
1000 × 800mm

Northern Irish artist, Stephen Johnston, paints his aging
father in this heartfelt, hyperrealist portrait. After recently
becoming a parent, Johnston was inspired to reflect on
his relationship with his own father and the love a parent
has for their child. He explains further: 'In its simplicity,
the painting quietly speaks of the connections that define
us, bridging the past and present in a timeless reflection
of the love and understanding that binds generations'.

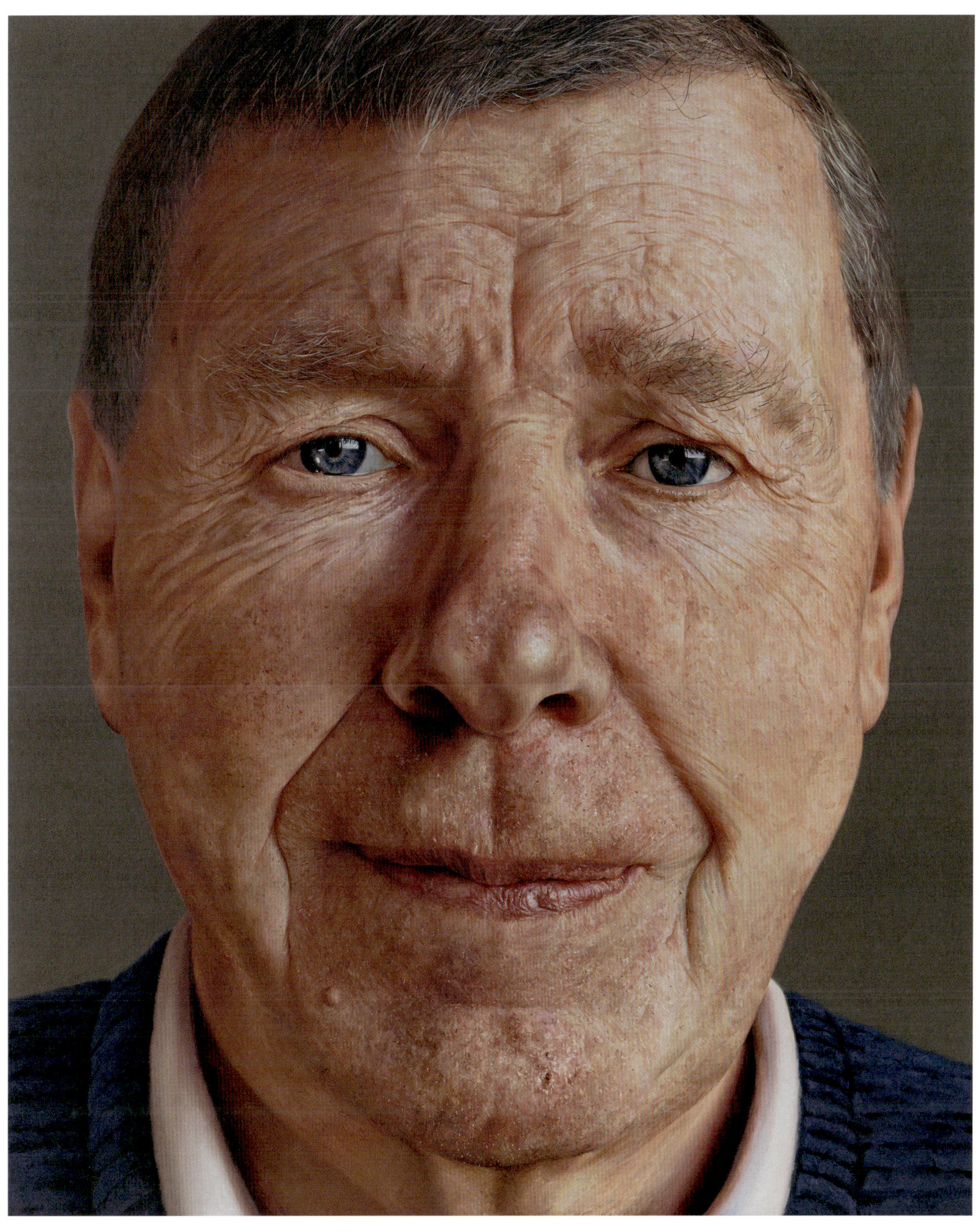

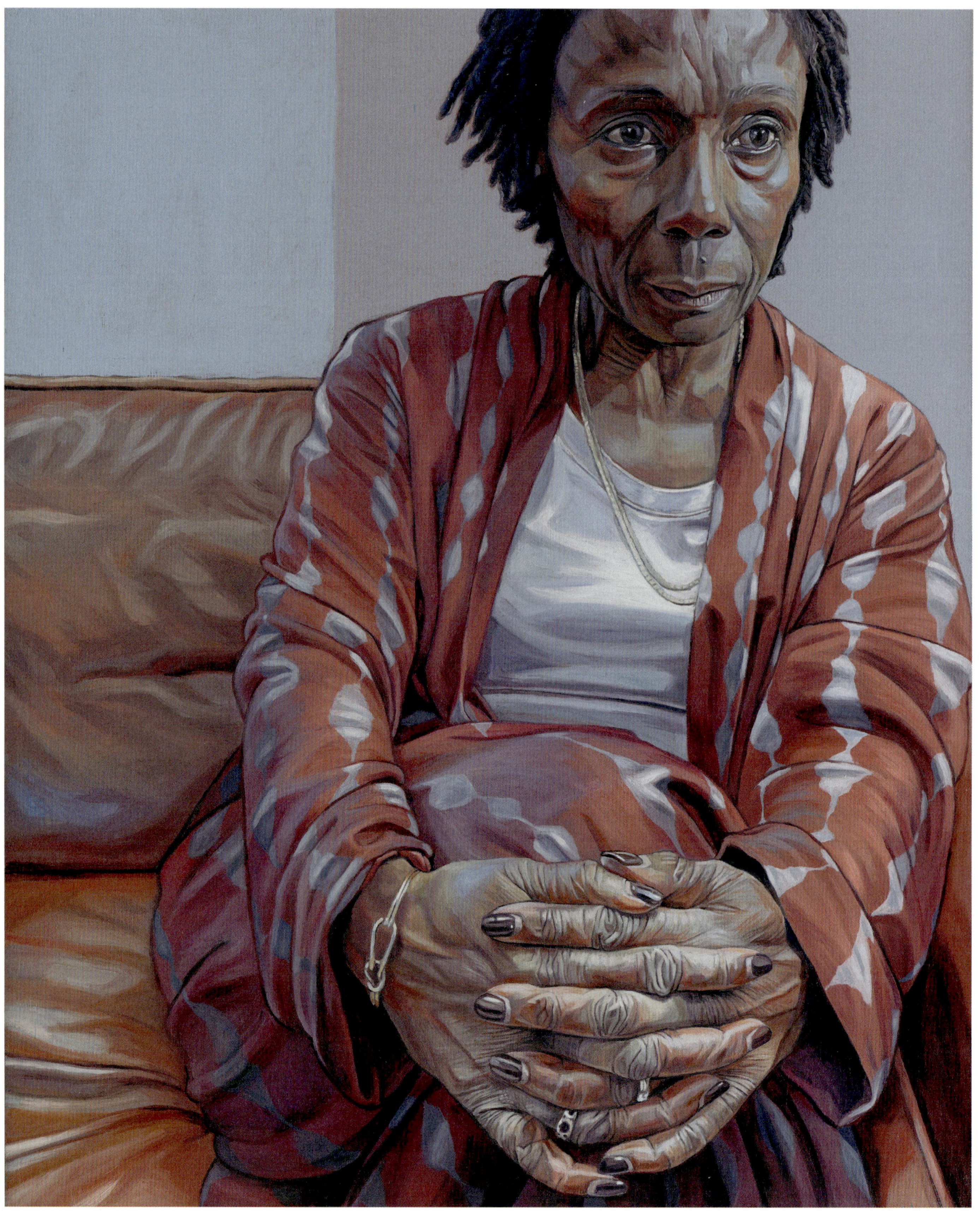

Peter Field
*Yeside*, 2023
Oil on board
510× 410mm

When making this portrait, Peter Field wanted to reflect his friend and fellow artist Yeside's strong and purposeful character. They spent several hours together in Yeside's home on the day of the sitting, trialling different poses and lighting. Yeside chose to wear a red and lilac dyed robe and eventually assumed the pose without direction. The artist intentionally gave prominence to her hands, which he felt were just as expressive as her face.

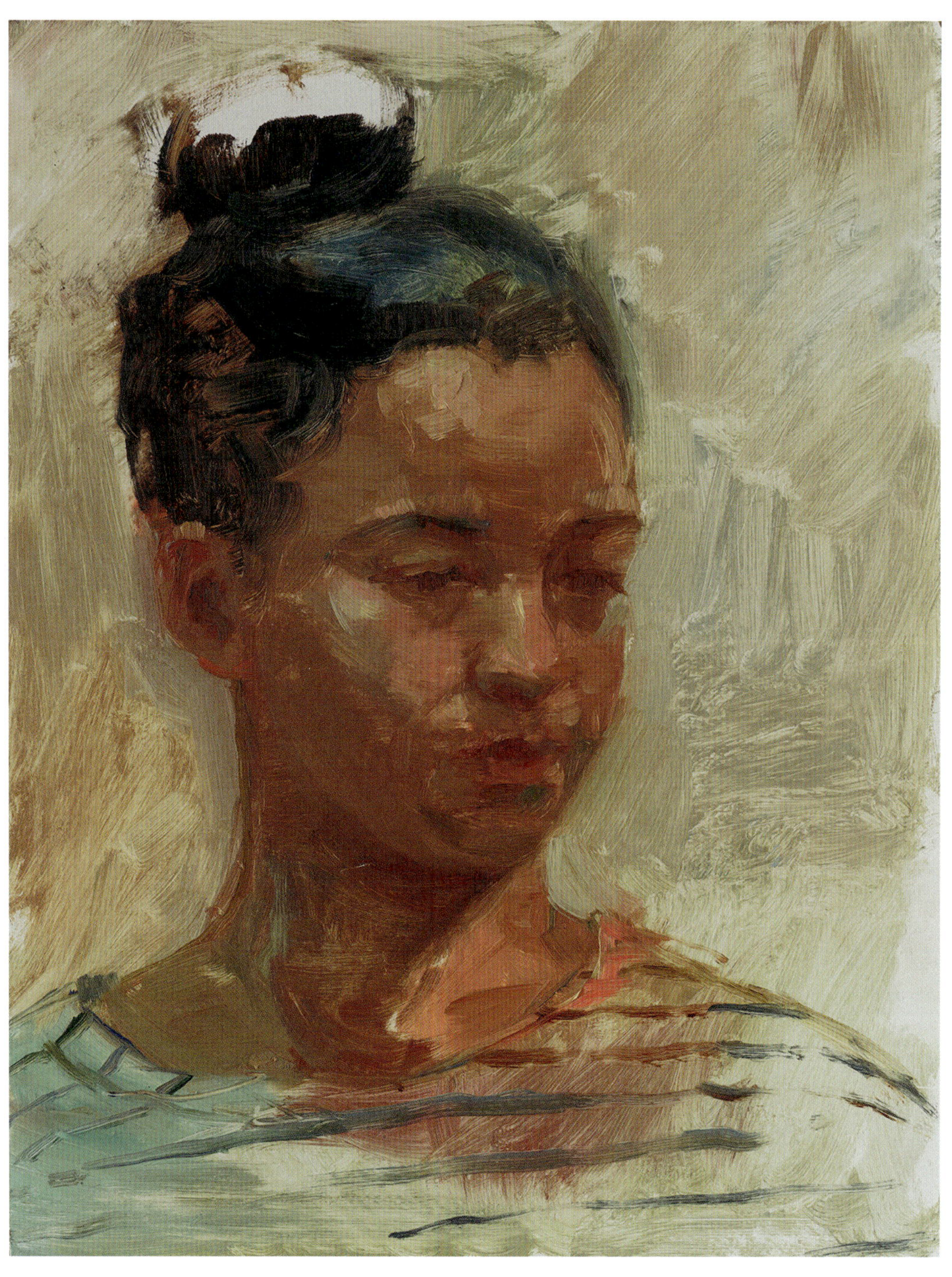

Ilaria Rosselli Del Turco
*Vanessa*, 2022
Oil on panel
290 × 235mm

Italian artist, Ilaria Rosselli Del Turco, painted this portrait with intense focus in less than one hour. Struck by the peculiar artificial lighting while teaching a painting class, the artist was inspired to buy a small board to paint Vanessa before returning to her class. Del Turco's familiarity with the sitter, having painted Vanessa for a decade, helped her to achieve a likeness quickly and focus instead on creating a warm and serendipitous image.

Emily Ponsonby
*Chewing the Cud*, 2023
Beeswax, oil and oil pastel on panel
1220 × 1560mm

*Chewing the Cud* captures three friends from rural Dorset immersed in a conversation that, according to Emily Ponsonby, 'snakes smoothly without being rushed and unravels at its own pace'. Using the tactile encaustic technique, Ponsonby scraped and stroked layers of pigment into the base of the painting made from honeyed wax, until the forms of the figures emerged. The artist then used oil pastel to build the composition further.

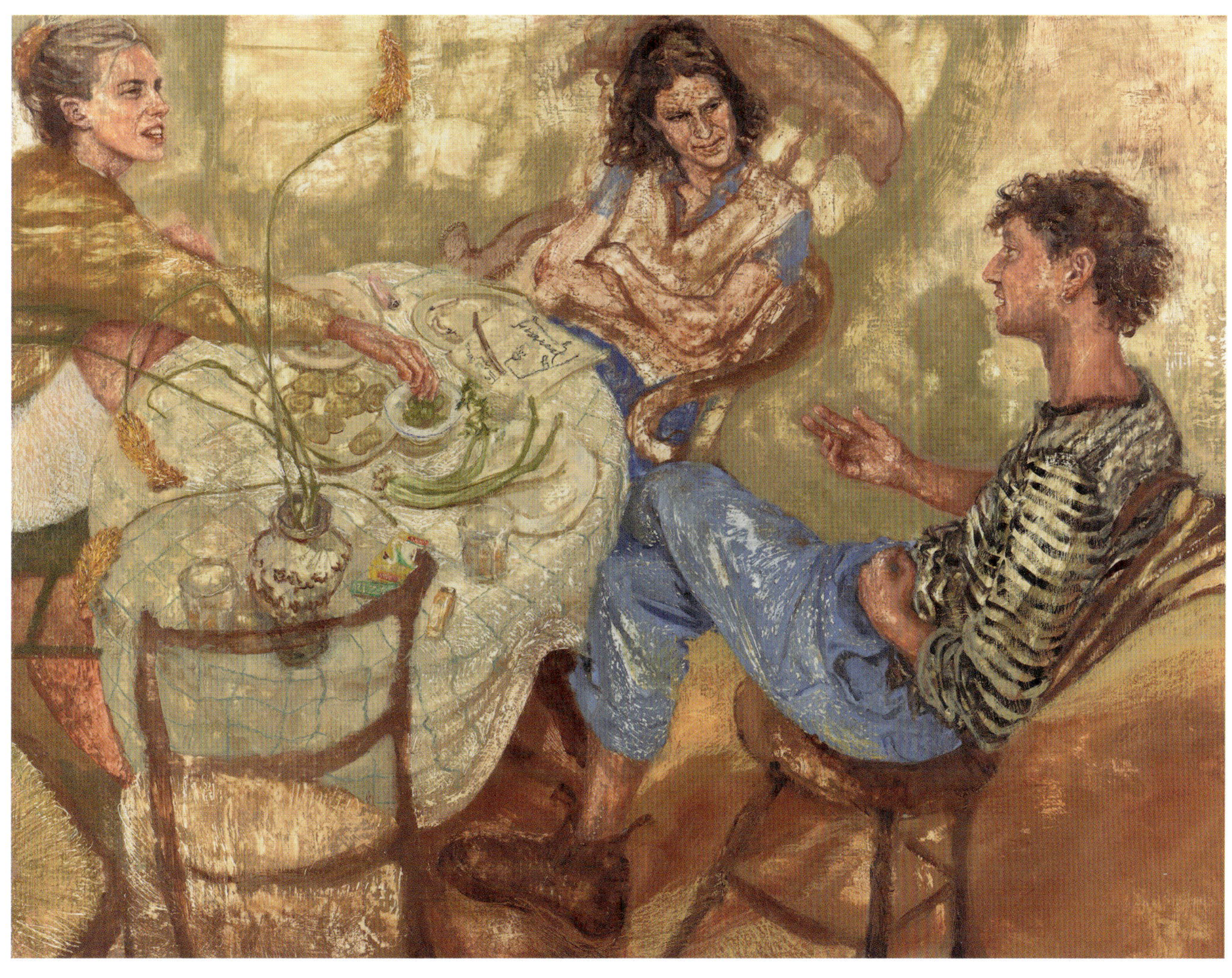

Alexander Macdonald
*Poppy*, 2023
Oil on canvas
740 × 540mm

Alexander Macdonald wanted to depict 'a strong young woman with a sense of optimism'. The sitter, Poppy, draws attention to her toad pendant necklace, a symbol of her love for her partner, the artist's son. The self-portrait in the background was exhibited in the National Portrait Gallery's Portrait Award in 1986. Based on more than twenty life sittings, this work marks the artist's return to the Portrait Award after almost forty years.

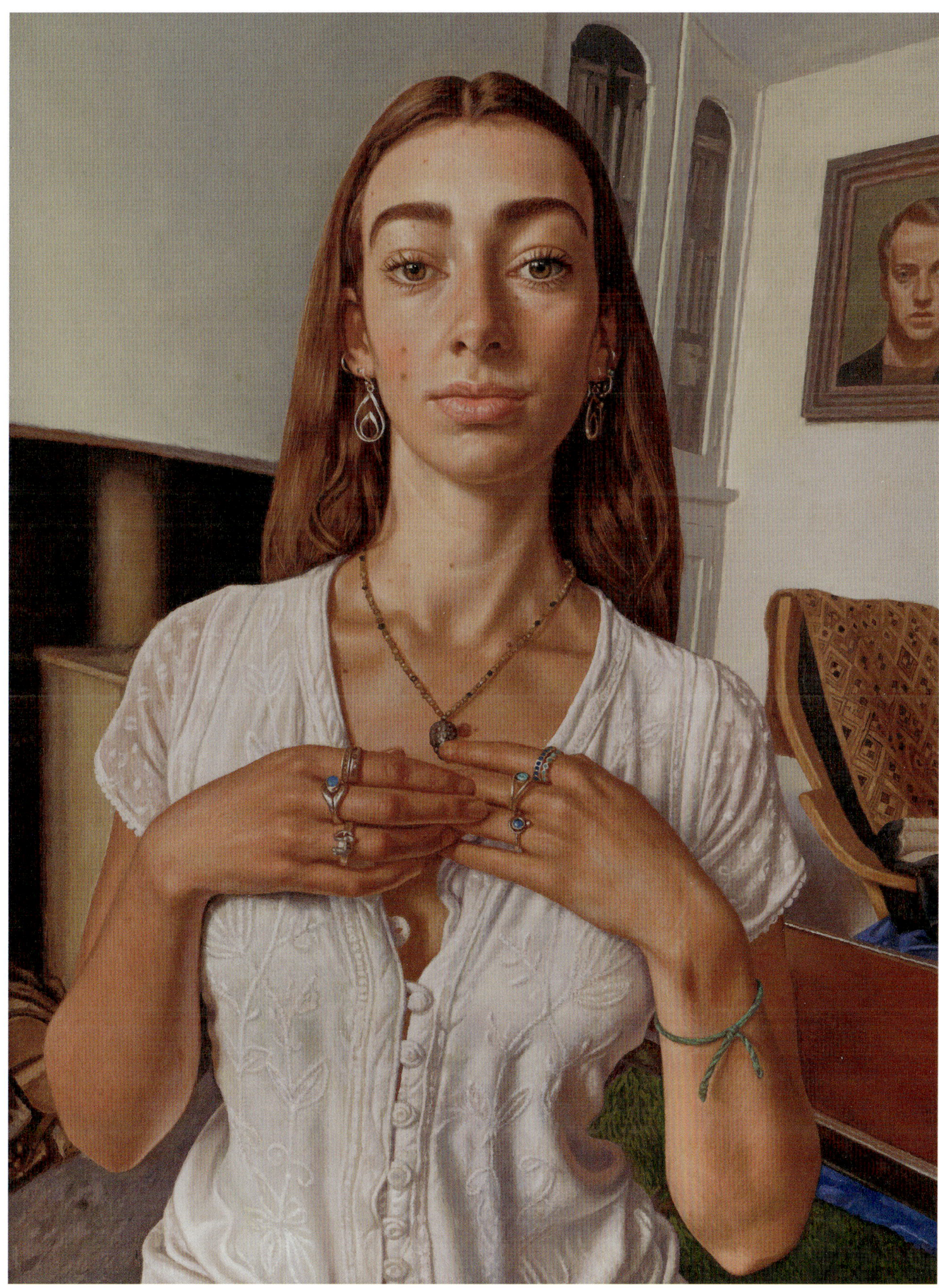

Jackie Anderson
*Gerard in Hospice*, 2023
Oil on cotton
600 × 660mm

Using only a few marks of near transparent brown paint, Scottish artist, Jackie Anderson, captures the weight of her husband Gerard's head, resting on a pillow. The artist made this painting in the last week of Gerard's life, creating a moving memorial to her dying husband. Anderson said: 'I wanted to capture how beautiful and peaceful he looked. It felt like the portrait painted itself.'

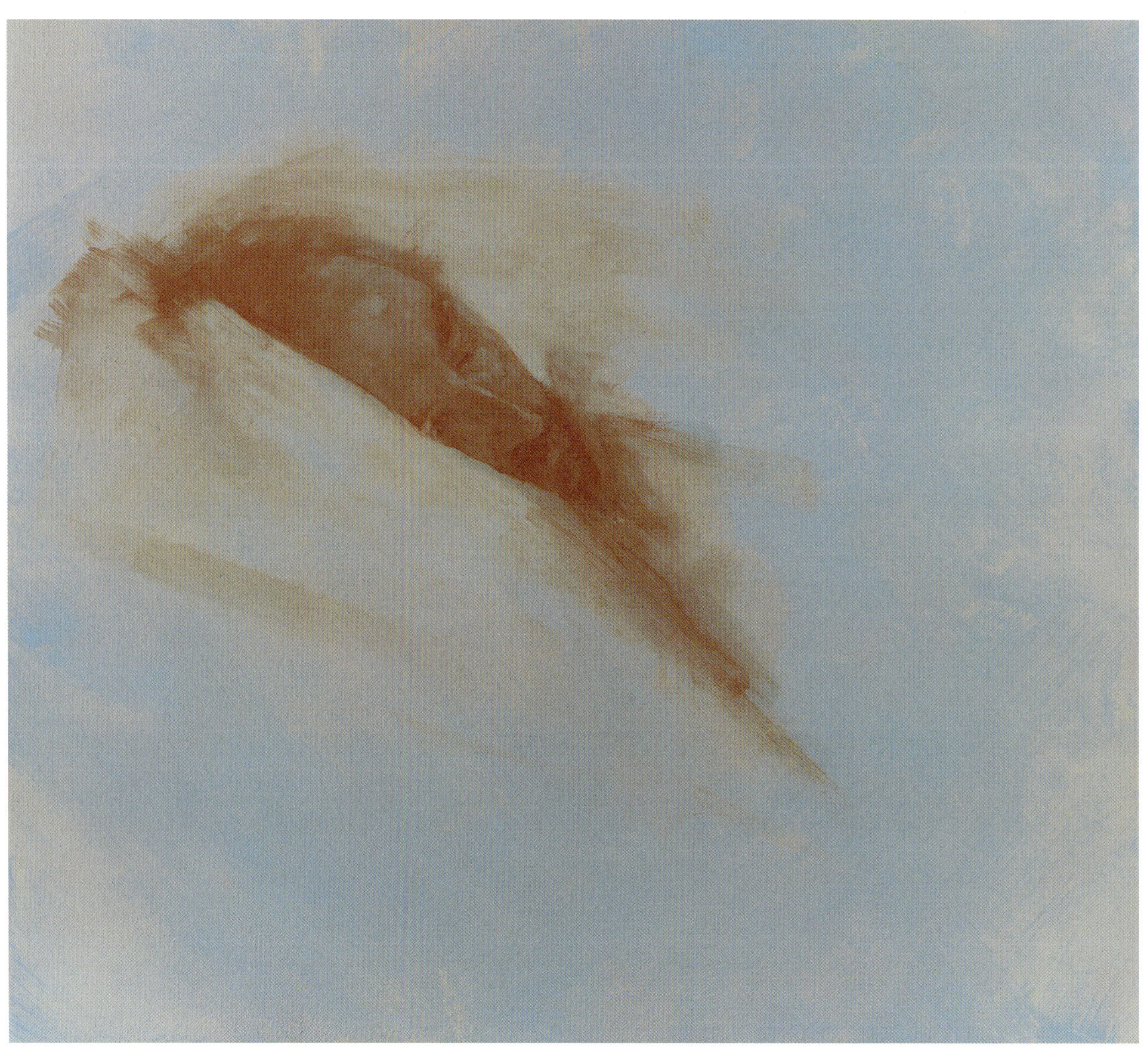

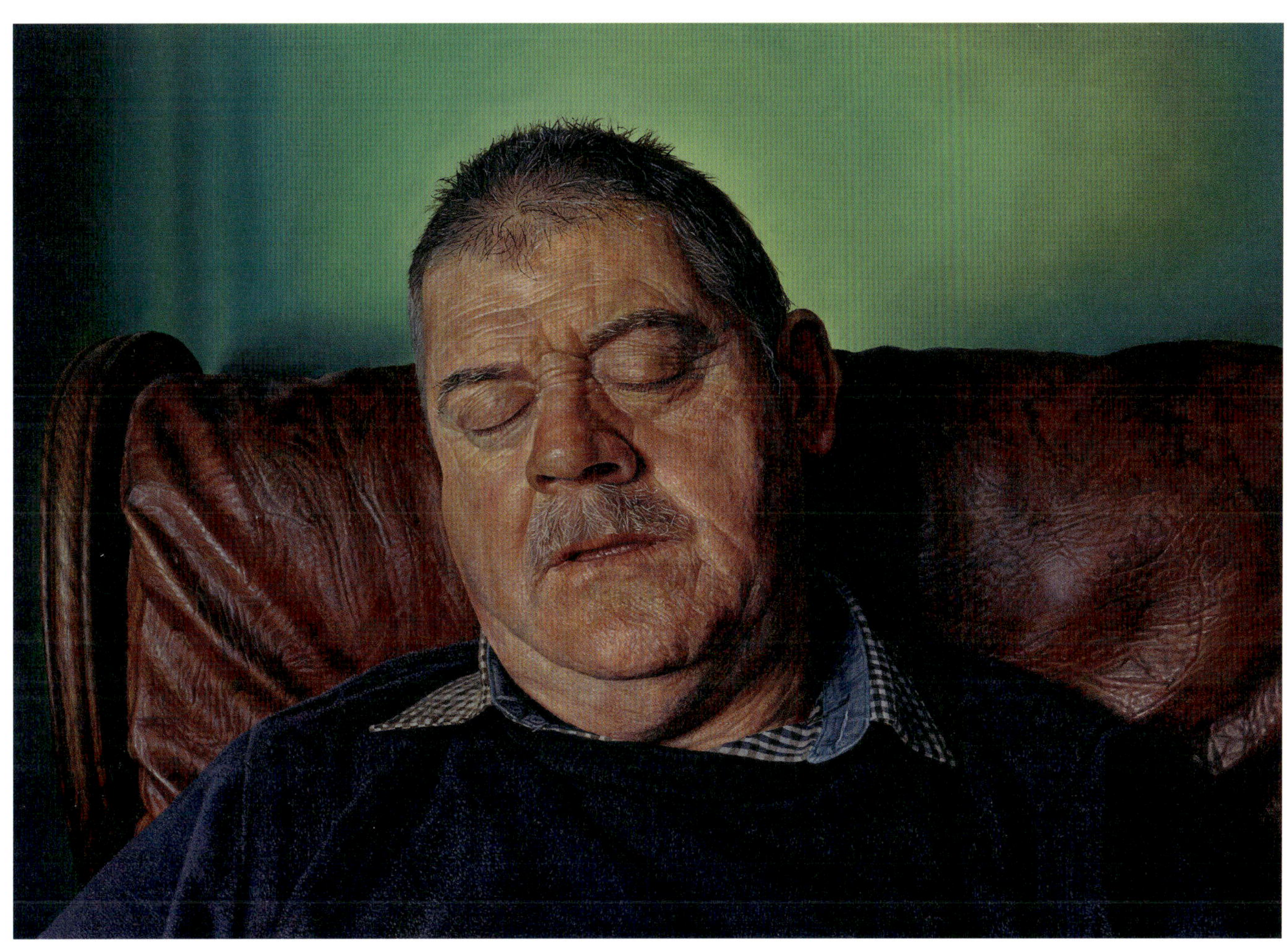

Daniel Nelis
*Man with Closed Eyes*, 2020
Oil on panel
210 × 290mm

Artist Daniel Nelis prefers to paint people and places that he knows. This work is of his father in a moment of unguarded honesty in his childhood home. Nelis lived with his father during the painting's creation, and this familiarity dispelled some of the self-awareness that can accompany more formal portrait sittings. Although on a small scale, the work is meticulously painted; the leather on the couch is rendered with a similar level of intense scrutiny as the figure.

Gabriel Lewis
*Shannice, Florentine Woman*, 2023
Oil on canvas
600 × 500mm

Gabriel Lewis painted this striking and classical portrait
from life over seven sittings. He uses the 'sight-size' method
taught at the Charles H. Cecil Studios, Florence, Italy,
where he was studying. This method involves placing
the sitter and canvas side by side. The artist then takes
several strides back in order to view the subject from a
distance. The technique was popularised by the Edwardian
portrait painter John Singer Sargent. The sitter, Shannice,
is an African-Italian illustrator who works in Florence.

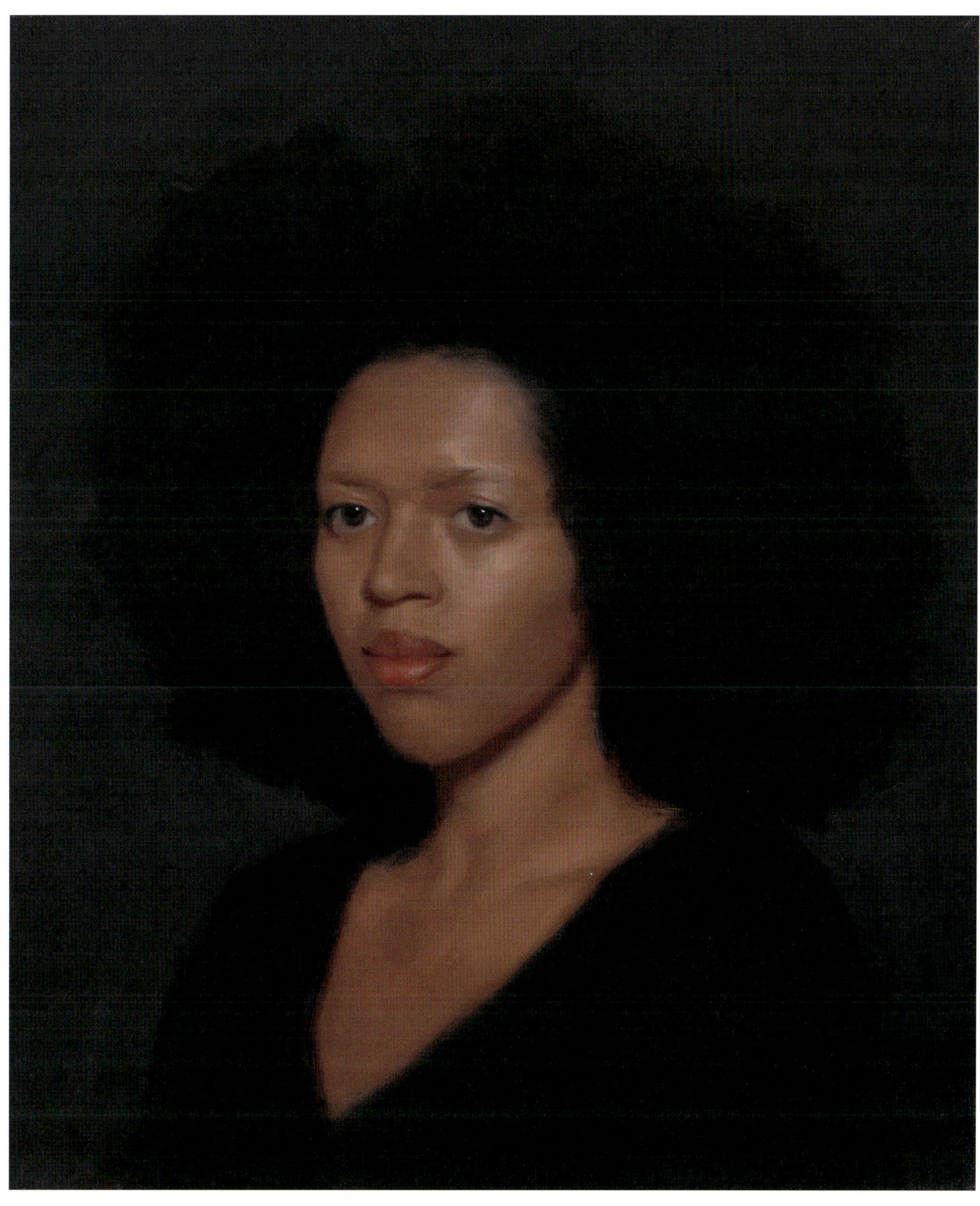

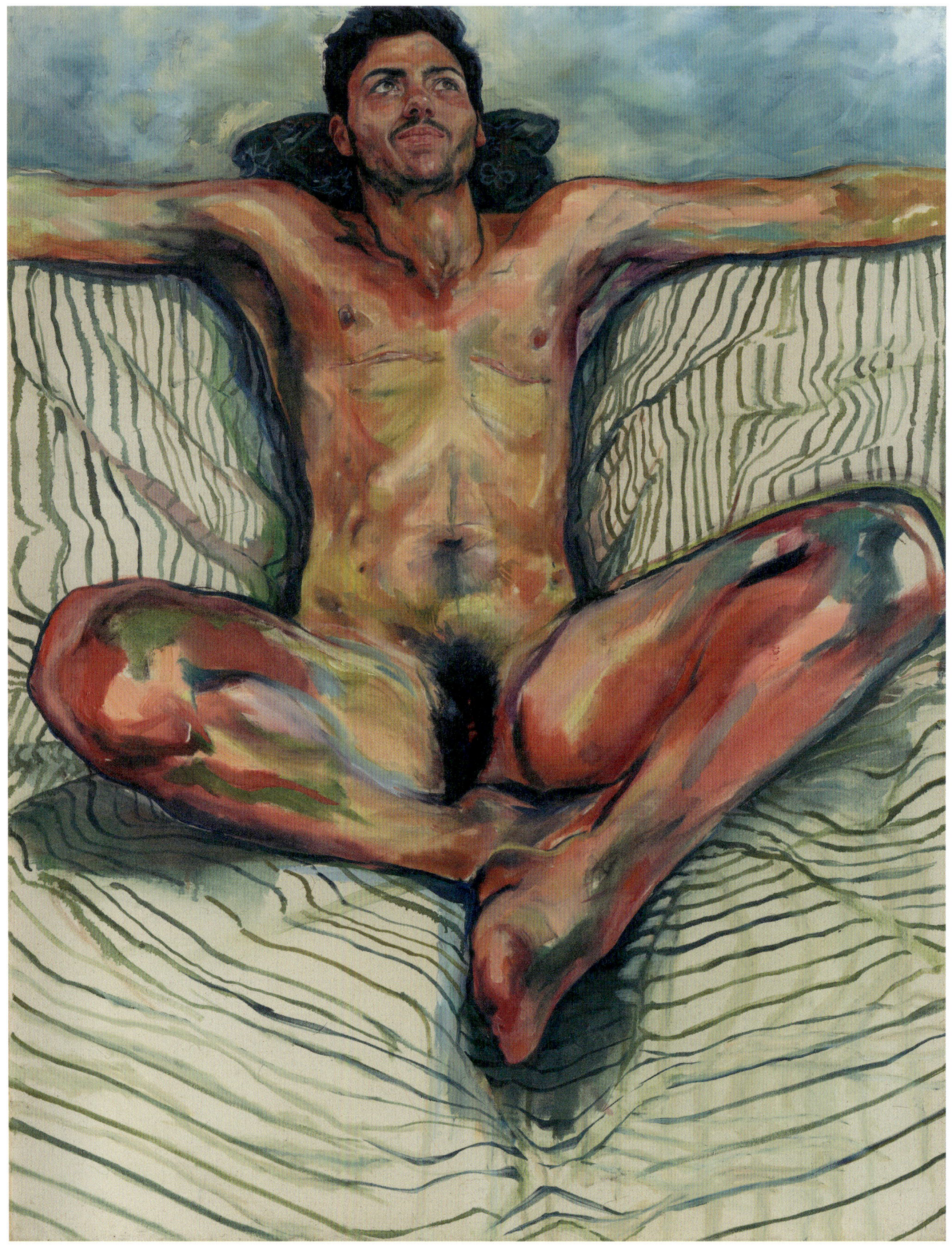

Marina Renée-Cemmick
*Many Lives, Many Bodies*, 2022
Oil on canvas
1200 × 800mm

Marina Renée-Cemmick created this portrait of her friend
to record his gender transition journey. During the sittings,
they listened to Martha Beck's *The Way of Integrity* (2021),
a book about finding a path to one's true self. The artist
recalled painting very quickly, 'marking the colours of the
body in an almost frantic way, finding the lights and tones
of the skin so gorgeous and my attempt to capture them
unsatisfactory but compelling.' The suggestion of the sky
in the background is imaginary, but perhaps points to the
sitter's hopes for the future.

Comhghall Casey
*Self-Portrait*, 2022
Oil on canvas
330 × 216mm

Irish artist, Comhghall Casey, has been making at least one self-portrait a year since he was a teenager. The series, now numbering over fifty closely observed, frank portraits, records the physical and mental processes of aging. The self-portraits, which are all made from life using a mirror, also reflect his developing technical abilities and confidence as an artist.

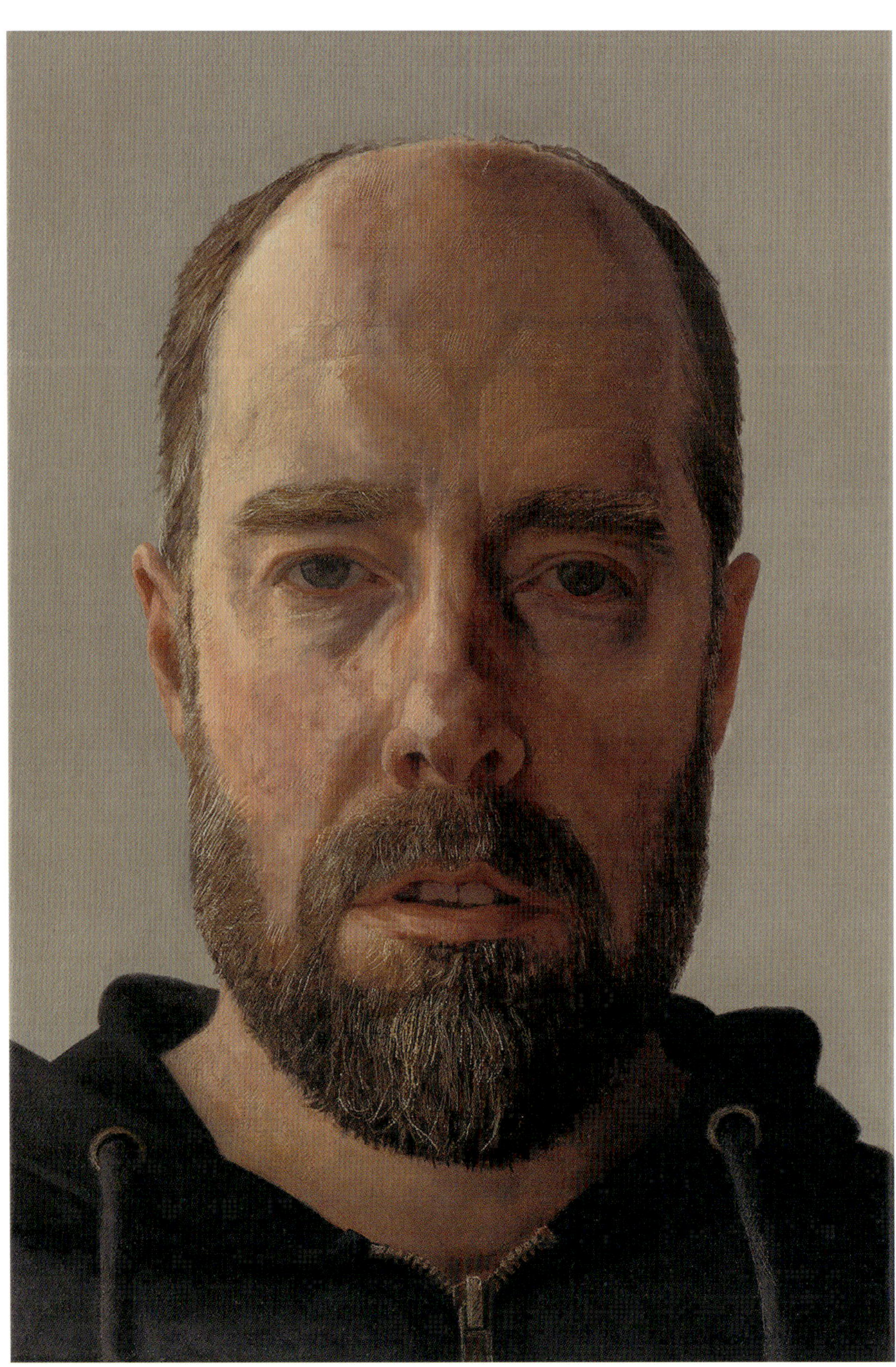

Estelle Day
*Self-Portrait in Studio V*, 2024
Oil on board
250 × 200mm

This small scale and intricately painted self-portrait took one year to make. British artist Estelle Day paints self-portraits regularly to capture herself in a particular moment, reflecting both her physical and emotional state. The background of the painting shows her studio filled with eclectic treasures that she has been collecting since childhood. Still life painting is another key passion for the artist and these personal objects are central to these works.

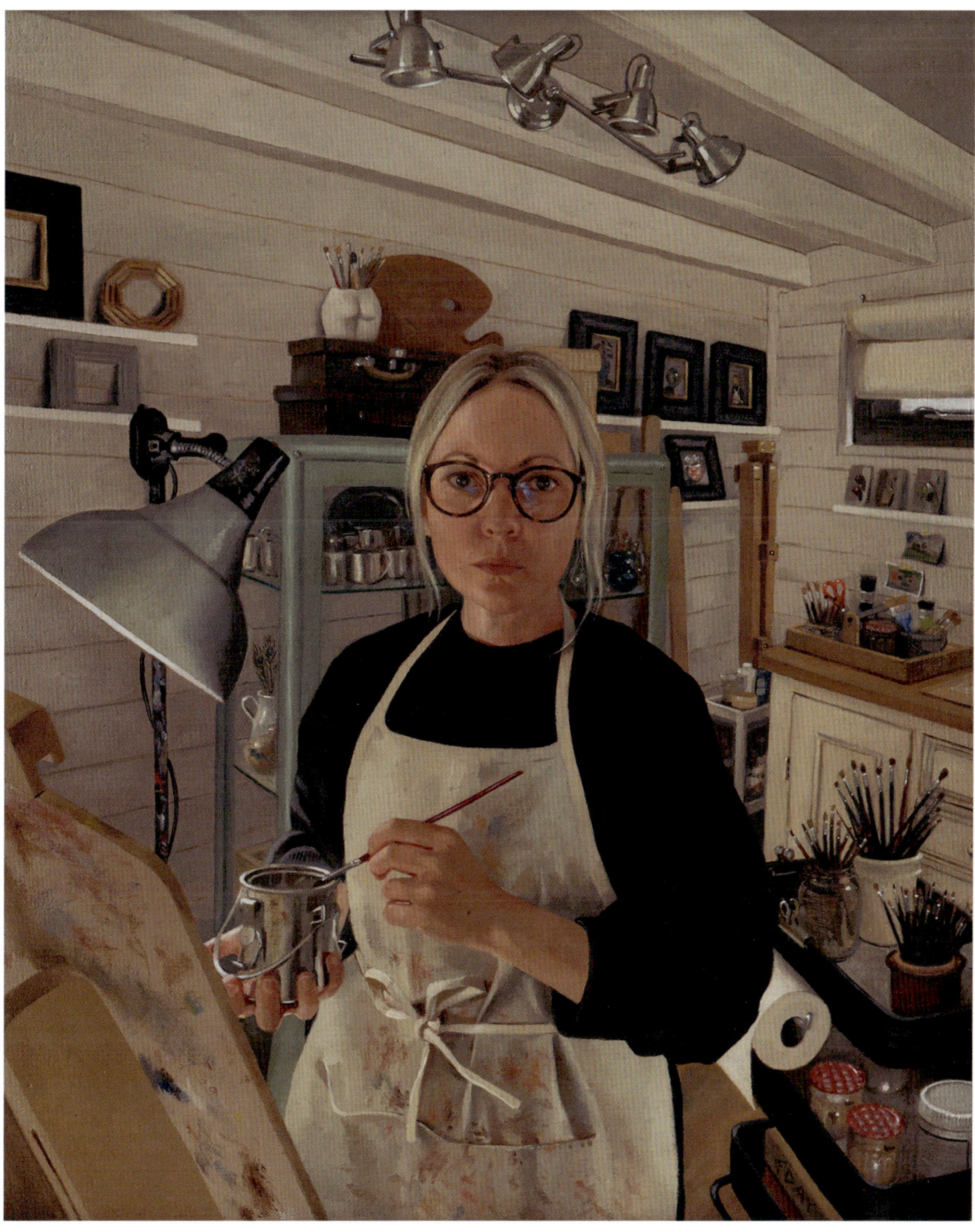

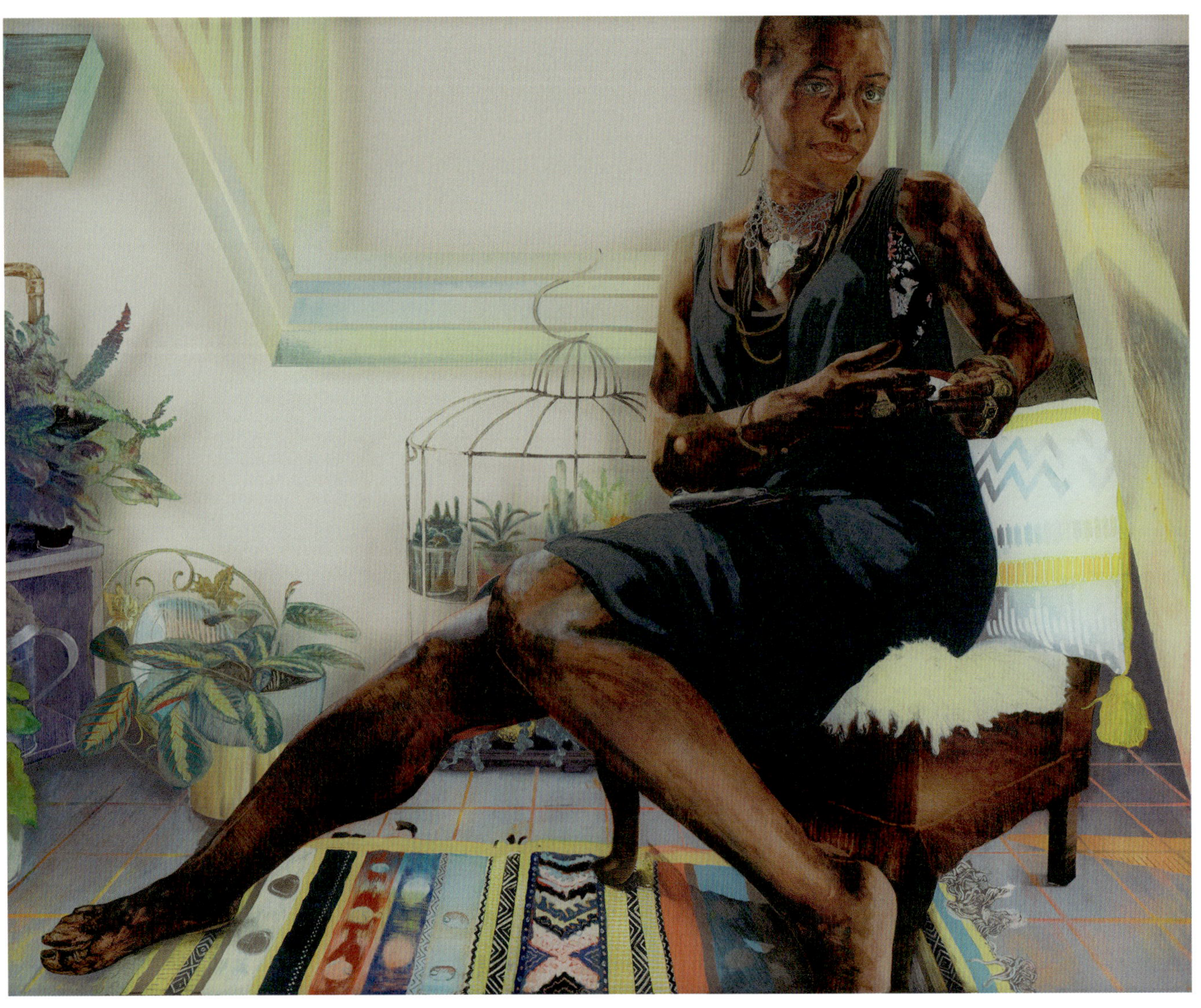

Oliver Bedeman
*T'Nia Miller*, 2024
Reverse oil on glass
1000 × 1200mm

T'Nia Miller is a British actor known for her roles in TV
shows such as *The Fall of the House of Usher* (2023),
*The Peripheral* (2022) and *The Haunting of Bly Manor*
(2020). Oliver Bedeman reached out to T'Nia through
Instagram and arranged a sitting at her home where
he made drawings and reference photographs. The
finished work is reverse painted on glass, which requires
the details and highlights to be painted first, in this case
T'Nia's eyelashes.

Zhang Yafei
*Grandmother*, 2024
Oil on canvas
500 × 400mm

Using classical painting techniques, Chinese artist, Zhang
Yafei, pays homage to his 'kind and strong' grandmother,
who had just returned home from hospital. Painting the
work allowed him to express 'the power of family affection'
and his gratitude towards her. In the background, Yafei
includes the landscape of his grandmother's hometown.
Resting on the table in the foreground is a wildflower
along with a gourd scoop and small broom, tools used
to make bread and noodles.

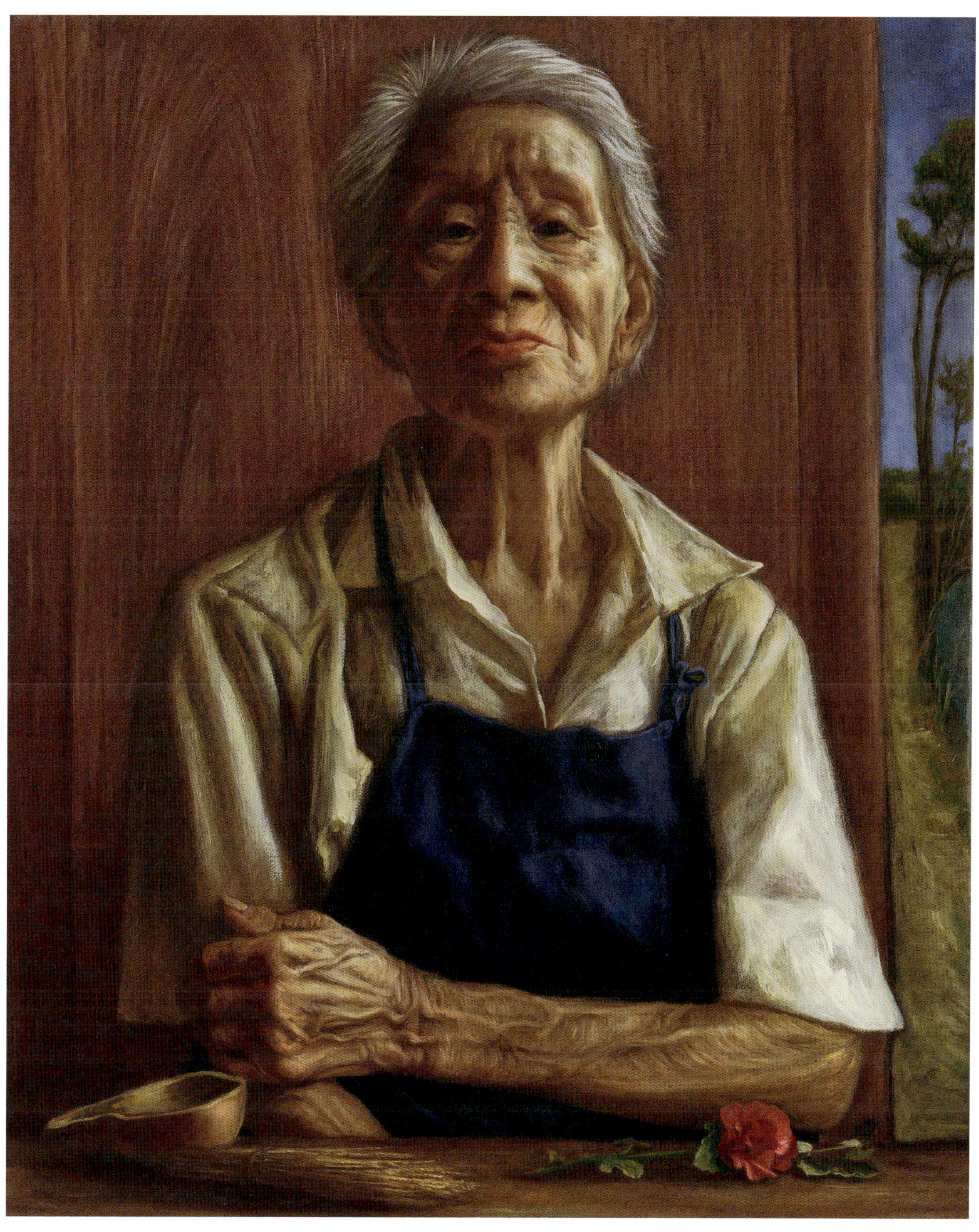

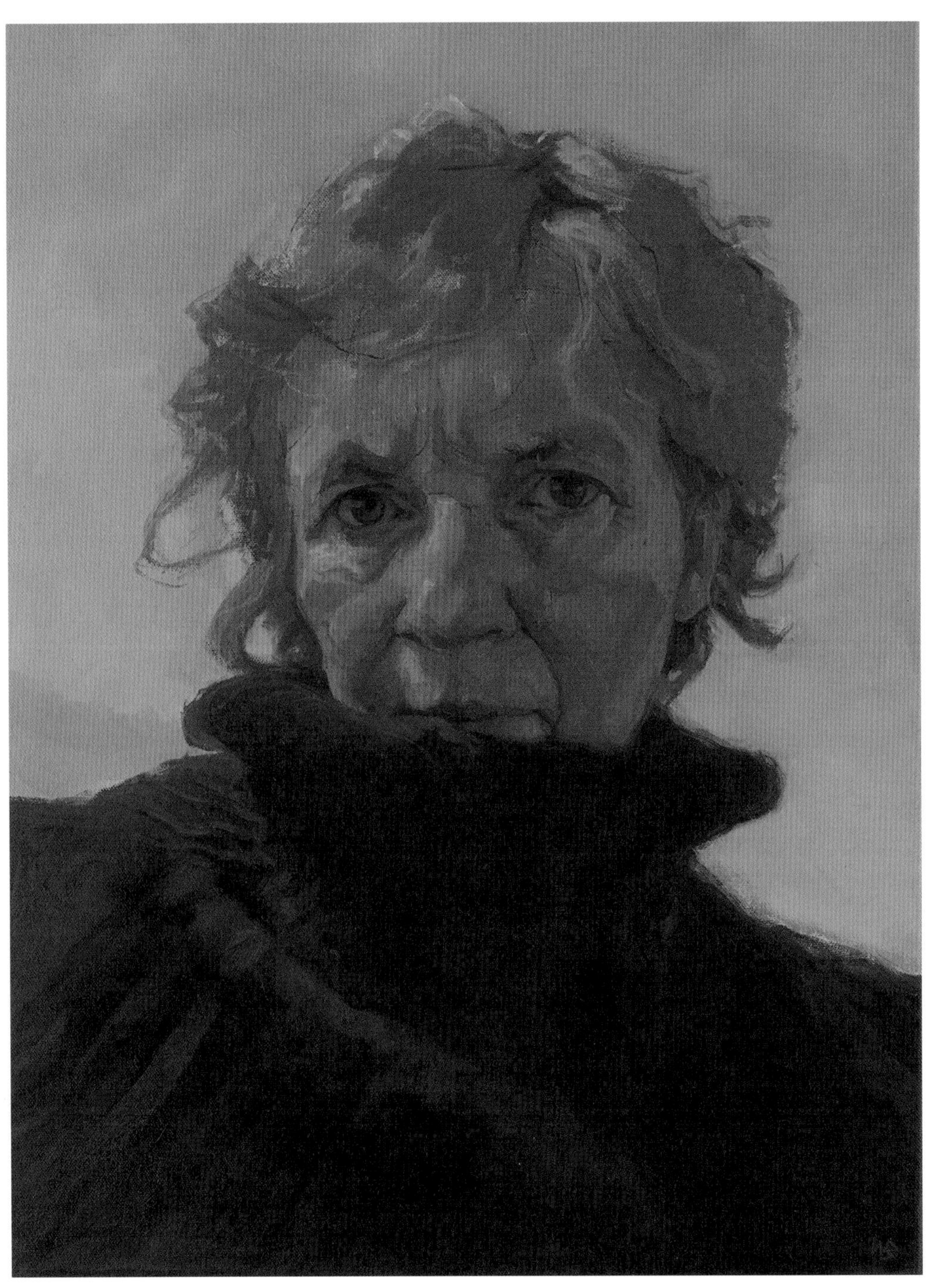

Wendy Barratt
*Self*, 2022
Oil on canvas
555 × 455mm

This is the second time this self-portrait has been shortlisted for a major painting competition. The first was for *Sky Portrait Artist of the Year 2023*. Wendy Barratt holds a tentative expression, with her neck burrowed into her knitted jumper as she awaits the critic's verdict. Barratt made a preliminary drawing directly onto the canvas, later adding final touches of more fluid lines using a fine rigger brush to emphasise certain colours and tones.

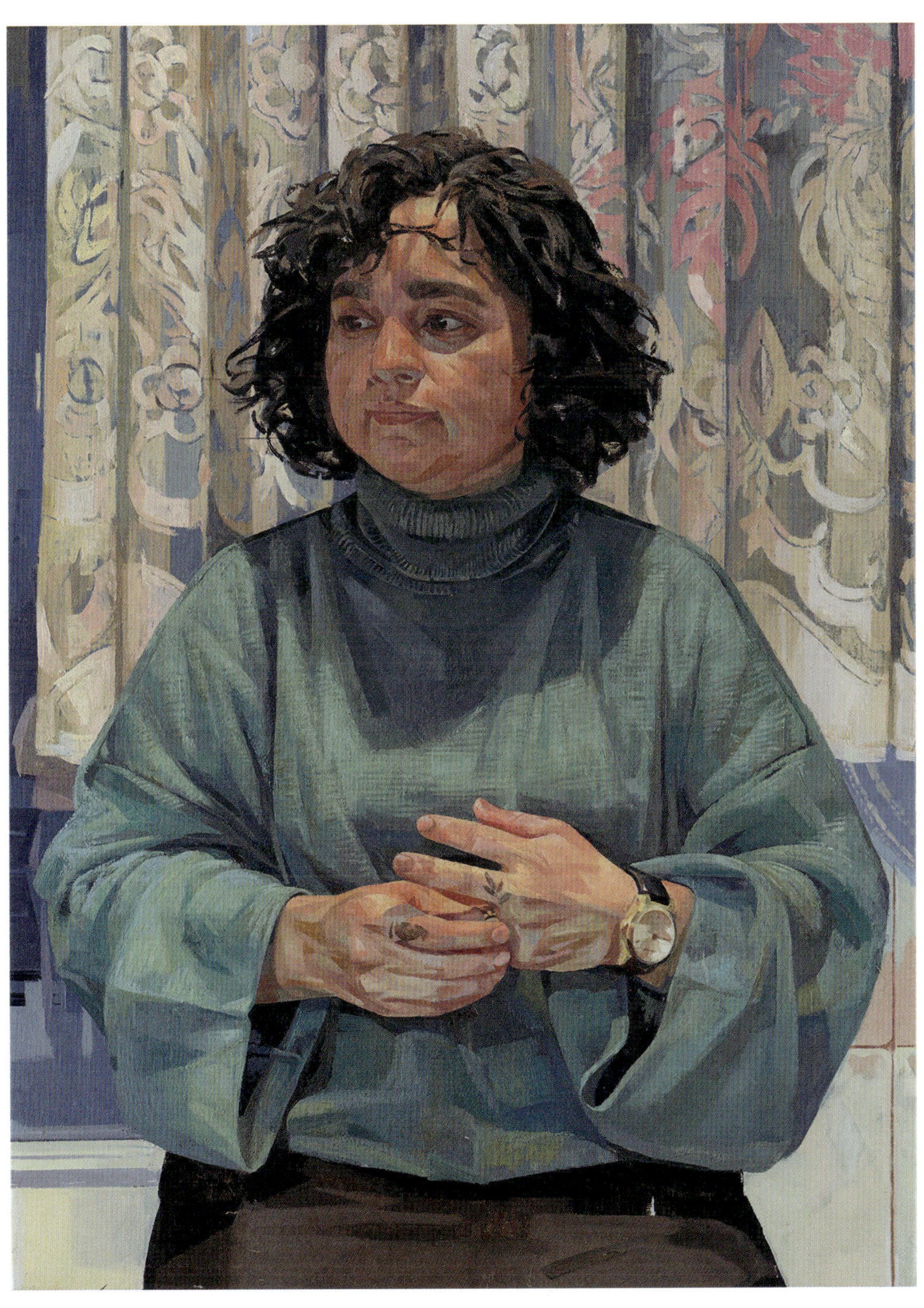

Hanie Soltani
*The Ring*, 2023
Oil on board
700 × 500mm

*The Ring* captures Hanie Soltani's close friend in a moment of introspection. The portrait focuses on the sitter's hands as she fiddles with her ring. This gesture infers the significant life decisions occupying her thoughts. The artist aims 'to explore universal truths and human experiences that resonate with everyone.' The painting was created at night using artificial light to set the mood.

Ashley Ogilvy
*I Am Because You Are*, 2023
Oil on panel
1160 × 915mm

Artist Ashley Ogilvy describes her sitter, who is a close
friend of their son, as a young man of 'great poise and
intelligence'. The shirt he wears in the portrait was a
gift from his future mother-in-law for his wedding day.
She added bands of a traditional cotton fabric called
shweshwe to the shirt edges as a reminder of his
Zimbabwean heritage. The title, *I Am Because You Are*,
is an English translation of the foundational proverb of
the African Ubuntu philosophy, which emphasises shared
responsibility and interconnectedness with community.

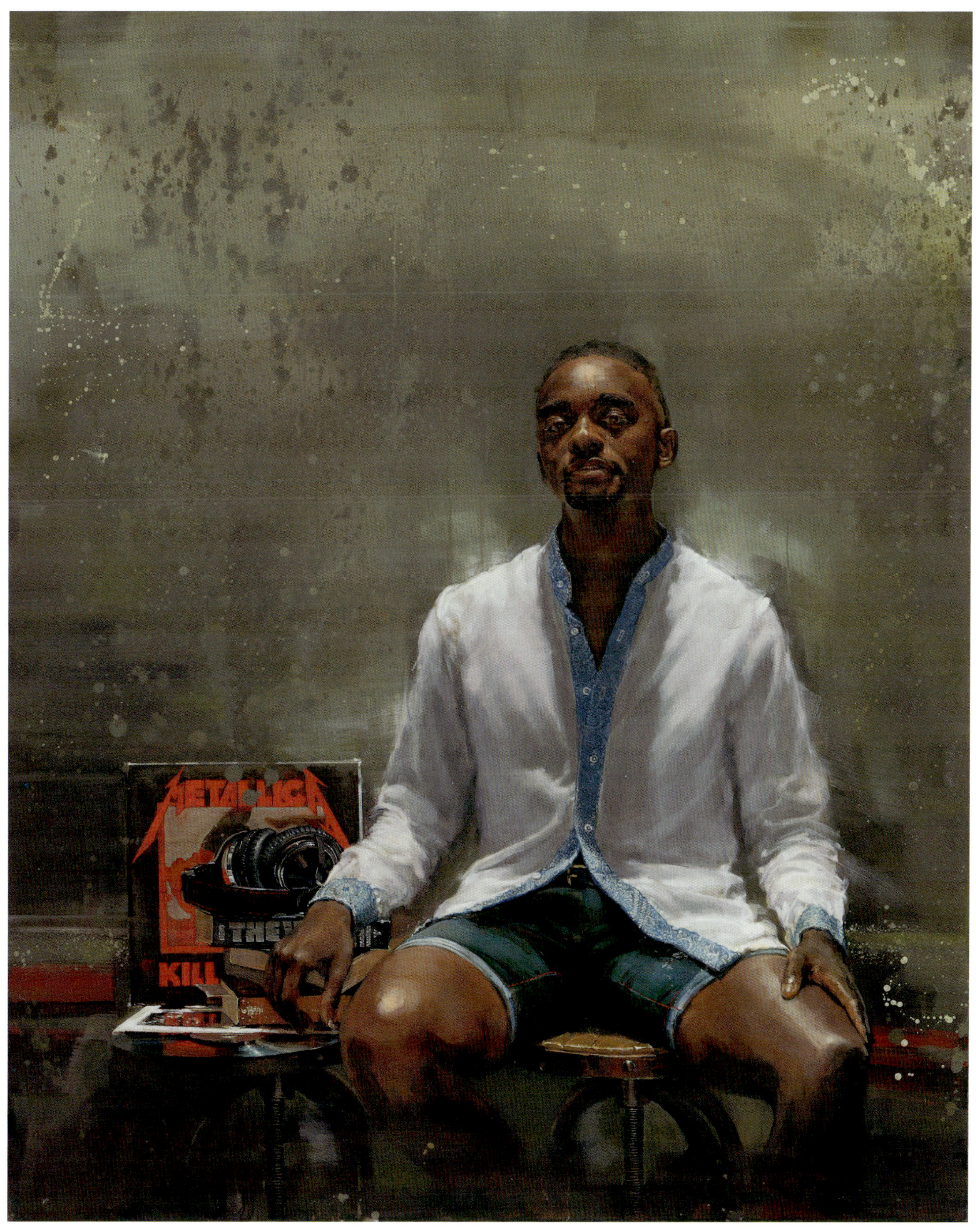

METALLICA
KILL

Published in Great Britain by
National Portrait Gallery Publications
National Portrait Gallery
St Martin's Place
London WC2H 0HE

Published to accompany the
*Herbert Smith Freehills Portrait Award 2024*

Exhibited at the National Portrait Gallery, London
from 11 July to 27 October 2024

Every purchase supports the National Portrait Gallery, London.

Information about the exhibition, competition and technical
information can be found at www.npg.org.uk/hsfportraitaward




ISBN 978 1 85514 544 3

A catalogue record for this book is available from the
British Library.

The Director of the National Portrait Gallery would like to thank
Poppy Andrews, Lydia Brightling-Reed, Emma Chiplin, Rachel
Dunlop, Andrea Easey, Kara Green, Jahnavi Inniss, Jemma
Jacobs, Priti Kothary, Ros Lawler, Francesca Laws, Gráinne
McCarthy, Gavin Nel, James O'Connell and the art handling
team, Abi Ponton, Charlotte Regan, Jessica Rutterford-Nice,
Jude Simmons, Alison Smith, Georgia Smith, Liz Smith, Anna
Starling, Eloise Stewart, Perry Stewart, Anna Sorrell, Oliver
Tratt, Denise Vogelsang, Saoirse Walsh, Helen Whiteoak, Natalia
de Wilde, Rosie Wilson and especially Clementine Williamson,
Exhibitions Manager, Sarah Morris, Exhibitions Officer, Callum
Brunton, Exhibitions Assistant, and Tanya Bentley, Contemporary
Curator, for their hard work on the project.

Director of Commercial and Operations:
Anna Starling
Senior Publishing Manager:
Kara Green
Production Manager:
Priti Kothary
Project Editor:
Jemma Jacobs
Design:
Peter Dawson, www.gradedesign.com

Origination by Altaimage London

Printed and bound in the UK by Park Communications

This publication is printed on FSC certified paper and has
been manufactured using 100% vegetable oil-based inks and
100% offshore wind electricity sourced from UK wind. Park
Communications Ltd is a carbon neutral production company.

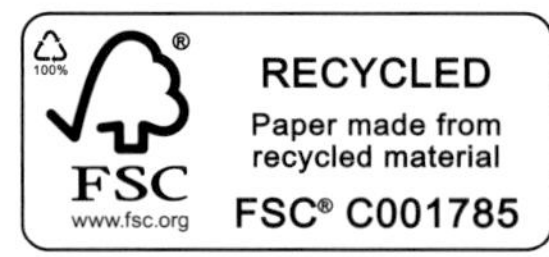